MW01055787

Globe Law
and Business

Negotiating Technology Contracts

Kit Burden, Mark O'Conor and **Duncan Pithouse**

Authors
Kit Burden, Mark O'Conor, Duncan Pithouse

Managing director
Sian O'Neill

Negotiating Technology Contracts
is published by

Globe Law and Business Ltd
3 Mylor Close
Horsell
Woking
Surrey GU21 4DD
United Kingdom
Tel: +44 20 3745 4770
www.globelawandbusiness.com

Printed and bound by CPI Group (UK) Ltd, Croydon CR0 4YY

Negotiating Technology Contracts

ISBN 9781787423220
EPUB ISBN 9781787423237
Adobe PDF ISBN 9781787423244
Mobi ISBN 9781787423251

Table of contents

Introduction

Technology contracts can be difficult things to negotiate. After all, if it was a straightforward and simple process, there would hardly be a need to write a book about it, and you wouldn't then be reading this introduction. However, that is not to say that you need to be the legal equivalent of a rocket scientist in order to be able to navigate safely and successfully through the negotiation maze. Instead, it is first and foremost a question of understanding the nature of the deal, the nuanced issues which it may then raise, and what then will be both the reasonable middle ground (or what might often be referred to as the 'market standard' positions) and the range of potential alternative provisions and compromises on either side of that line.

Our objective in this book is, therefore, to offer up a practical guide to the negotiation process, covering as broad a range of potential technology contracts as possible. Across the various chapters, we break down the contract into the key areas for potential negotiation, setting out in each case the nature of the issue and why it matters in the context of the wider contract. We then set out in turn the perspectives of both customer and service provider, and so seek to explain why each of them would want to set out the relevant provisions in what may be radically different ways, and so as to best protect their divergent interests. We trust that this will be helpful to people on both sides of the buy/sell divide, as we believe it is essential to understand where the other party is coming from if the customer or service provider are then to be able to identify potential compromises with them.

Accordingly, each chapter concludes by offering up our thoughts and observations as to potential solutions for the negotiation challenges which we have identified, based on our practical experience drawn from our collective 80 plus years of negotiations 'at the coal face', acting for both major customers and service providers in respect of their technology-related requirements and offerings, in both the private and public sector, and in jurisdictions all around the world.

It is not, therefore, our intention that this be a particularly legal book. Although we obviously focus on contract drafting and (very occasionally) even mention legislation or case law, our focus is very much on helping to facilitate the deal-making process. Ultimately, the positions which are reached are more a reflection of the commercial requirements and bargaining leverage of the parties as opposed to whether something can be said to be 'right' or 'wrong' from a legal perspective. Where the customer or service provider ends up in their real world negotiations will hopefully, therefore, be assisted by what is read in this book, not least in building an appreciation of what lies within the art of the possible in terms of alternative positions, but the knowledge imparted in these pages will be no substitute for gaining a full appreciation of the nature of the underlying deal and the true commercial needs of the respective contracting parties.

We are all recognised by the various legal directories as being leaders in the field of IT/outsourcing contacting, and work within the global technology and sourcing team of DLA Piper, the pre-eminent technology law practice. The views and suggestions in this book are, however, our own (and we reserve the right to run divergent arguments and remind you that there is no objective, single correct outcome in technology contract negotiations, should we ever turn up across the negotiation table to you!).

We hope you enjoy the book.

Kit Burden
Mark O'Conor
Duncan Pithouse
DLA Piper

1. Due diligence in outsourcing arrangements

1. Introduction

1.1 Overview of due diligence

Due diligence is the process of assessment of available information relating to the proposed project, where such information is necessary to ascertain before entering into an agreement (as will frequently be the case in longer-term deals or where the service provider is being asked to take on operations or assets from the customer, as in the case of an outsourcing project). It is an essential part of the pre-contract process because each party needs to know what they are getting into. The degree of due diligence undertaken by both parties prior to entering into an agreement can determine the success of the ongoing relationship (and equally, lack of suitable due diligence is often a factor in a project's failure).

As such, the due diligence from the customer perspective will be intertwined with the outsourcing process, particularly in a competitive process whereby the act of bid evaluation and negotiation will help to prove the ability of the service provider to meet the needs of the customer. But the due diligence by the customer is not only a process of service provider assessment; the customer must also be clear on its own requirements and deal context, and as such the customer needs to perform a degree of self-analysis. By contrast, the due diligence to be performed by the service provider will be to interrogate the customer's requirements and all associated factors such as the customer's legacy technology estate and stakeholder attitudes, and could even include assessment of the customer's customers, be they consumers or end-users so as to understand their attitudes and requirements for the new service provision.

Failure to undertake a suitable amount of due diligence risks the customer and service provider entering into an agreement with only partial information; essentially leaping blind into a contractual arrangement, meaning that inevitably matters will play-out differently to that expected, causing frustration and surprise, and risking the anticipated commercial balance of the deal. That means that either the customer will contract with a service provider which is not what it thought it was, or the service provider will seek to provide a solution for a customer which does not quite fit. The end result of this is post-contract renegotiation, often combined with accusations of bad faith, changes in solution and price and potential deal failure.

1.2 Factors affecting the extent of due diligence conducted

How far the investigation goes will depend upon numerous deal factors, including:

- in the case of an outsourcing style arrangement, whether the outsource is a first-time outsource (in which case the customer may have a good amount of information as to the current service it self-provides, but, firstly, will not necessarily want the service provider to replicate that service and, secondly, may struggle to detail elements such as current levels of service because they are simply not measured);
- the availability of relevant information;
- the extent to which the customer is prepared to make that information available (even if information is available);
- the extent to which a customer's requirements are bespoke (meaning that the new requirements are so different to the current service that due diligence on the current service is a waste of time);
- the time available in the negotiation/procurement process for due diligence to occur at all;
- the extent to which due diligence is normal for the sector (for example, often a financial services or public sector standard template contract seeks to put the risk of due diligence onto the service provider entirely and seeks to prevent any post-contract variation – where that is the case, then it is normal for a due diligence process to be undertaken by poten-tial service providers in parallel to the competitive request for proposal (RfP) process);
- what the customer is buying (whether an input, required output or new outcome) will influence the relevance and extent of due diligence;
- whether the customer is expecting the service provider to take over a function, or to transform a process completely, will again influence the extent to which due diligence is sensible; and

- the art of the possible – the commercial reality of due diligence as a process, its cost to both parties, the disruption it might cause, how exhaustive it needs to be and the time available.

Taking all of those factors together, a key principle emerges, and that is price certainty. Due diligence is undertaken by the service provider to ensure that it understands the requirements and customer environment, and is allowed by the customer to ensure that the service provider does not need to caveat its commercial response. All of these lead to greater certainty of pricing and should in turn avoid endless change control post-contract and the damage to the relationship between the parties that that will bring.

1.3 Contract certainty

It should be remembered that the basis for judicial interpretation (as summarised in *Rainy Sky SA v Kookmin Bank* [2011] UKSC 50; [2011] 1 WLR 2900) is business common sense. That means that, provided that the terms of an agreement are clear, a court will not interfere in its drafting, even if the deal is a poor deal, and instead will give effect to its terms.

This is relevant and important to remember because due diligence will afford both parties the opportunity to sense-check the deal they are about to enter into, the abilities of the counterparty to perform and wider commercial and economic factors which might be relevant.

At the end of the due diligence exercise, a typical contract makes clear that only the terms of that contract apply to the contractual relationship. This is the 'four corners' of the contract scope, and it is the negotiator's job, when drafting and negotiating the contract's terms, to ensure that those boundaries are clear and understood by both parties. Failure to do this correctly will, again, lead to uncertainty, cause debate and argument and threaten the success of the project. In particular, the formulation of a normal entire agreement clause will exclude prior agreements, negotiations and discussions and state that neither party has relied on statements made by the other. As such the message is clear. If a concept is sufficiently important, then it should be catered for in the express terms of the contract. If it is less important, has not influenced a party to enter into the agreement or is mere marketing material, then it should be excluded because it is likely to be written in language which is at odds with the terms of the contract and its schedules. This could lead to uncertainty.

1.4 Due diligence is correct at the time it is done

It is important to understand the limitations of due diligence. It is unlikely that the process can be completed with perfection by either party, and perfection is the enemy of good in this regard. As such the outcome is an understanding at a point in time, based on the best available information, which will feed into the internal business case sign-off process for both the service provider and customer. However, the only universal truth is that matters will not stay the same. As such, while minor changes can be absorbed and catered for, a major change (for example, a change in law, change in political backdrop, a catastrophic event affecting the supply chain) might fundamentally change the expected underpinnings of a contract.

While civil law countries, particularly across Europe, have variants of the 'hardship' principle (whereby a change in circumstance upon which the contract was based can, under certain circumstances, allow a party to go to court to seek an order to compel a contract change to reflect that change), such a principle does not exist in English law. Consequently, the express terms dealing with responsibility for due diligence (and its outcomes), and express terms dealing with the ways in which changes to an agreement can be requested (or mandated) become critical to apportioning the due diligence risk between the parties.

1.5 The due diligence process

In making information available, the customer will need to ensure that the information release is made in a controlled way. For example, information containing personal data may mean that disclosure will violate privacy policies and applicable data protection laws. Equally, disclosure could breach a third-party existing contract. Contracts may include terms that prohibit the parties from disclosing the terms or existence of the contract to other persons without the other party's consent. The customer will need to check the terms of its existing contracts prior to making them available. As such the information should be made available in a controlled way, covered by a duty of confidence (for example a non-disclosure agreement forming part of the terms and conditions applying to the RfP process itself) and with a clear mechanism for return of the data.

1.6 Types of due diligence information
There is no one-size-fits-all for due diligence because the details required will vary from contract to contract. Nonetheless there are several likely candidates for due diligence concepts which are liable to be relevant for most outsourcing projects. These will include:

- technical detail;
- prior performance;
- user attitudes and requirements;
- staff details;
- relevant premises and locations;
- provided assets, licences and technology; and
- contracts to be managed or transferred.

These concepts are explored from the customer and service provider perspective below.

2. The customer perspective
From the customer perspective due diligence involves two concepts:

- the due diligence that the customer will perform on the potential service provider and on itself; and
- the customer attitude to due diligence as encapsulated by the terms of the contract.

2.1 The due diligence the customer will perform
A customer will need to be sure that its chosen service provider is capable of providing a good service. Furthermore, the customer will need to be sure that the chosen service provider's solution will 'fit', by which is meant that the service provider's solution must be capable of user acceptance, both technically and culturally, so as to avoid 'tissue-rejection' by the ultimate end users of the service (be they consumers or customer employees). As such the types of due diligence which can and should (time permitting) be performed by the customer include the following.

- *Reputation and credentials.* A customer will want to know that the perceived service provider reputation is genuine. As such it will undertake site visits and seek references from other customers for similar solutions.
- *Financial.* A customer will seek input from external sources (for example, a credit ratings agency) to verify the financial status of the service provider. This will be essential if the agreement is of a substantial value, and for example, carries data and security risks which could lead to the customer making a claim.

It would be pointless securing excellent liability provisions if the service provider is financially incapable of standing behind those provisions.

- *Work in progress.* It may be that the customer wishes the service provider to take on certain in-flight projects. If so, the customer will need to perform due diligence on itself to ensure that these are captured in the requirements description.
- *Due diligence sufficient to write an RfP in such a way as to minimise assumptions and dependencies.* The more a customer can be precise about its requirements, technology and organisational environment, the less the supplier community will hedge their bid responses with assumptions and dependencies. Furthermore, if the customer can open the windows entirely to its organisation, current foibles and internal politics, as well as the more procedural matters of technology estate, then the customer should be in a better position to win the argument regarding due diligence risk transfer to the service provider. Such 'self-due diligence' must include:
  - *The current IT estate.* What assets, third parties, technology and licence terms surrounding the current service provision? Will these be passed onto the service provider? Will the service provider be expected to swap-out certain elements and bring its own solution? Will the service provider be expected to take on certain third-party arrangements and perform some sort of managed service using these elements of technology? If so, consideration will need to be given as to whether the contracts relating to such technology can be transferred to the service provider. The customer will need to be clear regarding the relevant assets, where they are actually situated and how far through their expected life they have gone. This is essential because the service provider, if asked to take on the ongoing maintenance of such assets, and use them for service provision, will need to know whether the assets are good enough, and how soon there will need to be a technology refresh of some or all of the estate. The customer team will also need to be clear as part of its business case whether those assets will be sold to the service provider, and whether any relevant product warranties can be passed onto the service provider.

- *The people.* Who performs the service now? Are they valuable people that the customer intends to reassign or are they a resource that the customer is seeking to cut?
- *The level of service.* Can the customer explain with precision the current level of service and is it intended that that level of service be preserved, or is the point of the outsource to improve the level of service?

2.2 The customer attitude to due diligence as encapsulated by the terms of the contract

From the customer perspective, due diligence concepts will manifest themselves in a due diligence clause itself, a sweeper clause and wording to deal with financial stability.

(a) Due diligence clause

A typical clause will fully transfer due diligence risk to the service provider. The service provider will be asked to acknowledge that it has conducted all necessary due diligence prior to the effective date of the agreement and that it will therefore be liable to perform the required services during the term without any ability to seek to vary its price or service provision, save where the customer agrees through the change control mechanism. Furthermore, it is common to deal with reliance risk expressly; stating that the service provider has entered into the agreement in reliance on its own due diligence, and has not relied on any representations, warranties or other information from the customer.

(b) Sweeper clause

The customer will endeavour to be exhaustive in its requirement specification, but it is likely that it will be impossible to detail every requirement. That said, from the customer perspective, the customer will be relying on the service provider's skill and experience to join the dots, and to anticipate reasonable additional elements. The typical analogy is to making a cup of tea; if the customer specifies a requirement for tea, including hot water, tea leaves, milk and sugar, but fails to specify the teapot and cup, the customer will, through the 'sweeper clause', seek to make the additional provision of the unspecified teapot and cup an expected part of the service provision. As such the 'sweeper clause' will make it clear that the service provider will also be responsible for additional obligations and aspects of the service which may not have been expressly stated, but which are reasonable to expect to form part of the customer's requirements.

(c)   ***No post-contract variation***
To put the matter beyond doubt, customers often include express wording to state that there is no ability for post-contract variation, even if new details come to light after the effective date.

(d)   ***Contractualise financial stability***
Together with the above clauses, many customers are concerned as to the ongoing financial viability of their service provider, particularly where they have outsourced critical functions. As such it is common for clauses to be included in the contract whereby the existing financial status of the service provider is recorded (perhaps by way of credit rating) and an obligation is imposed upon the service provider to monitor its own credit worthiness and inform the customer of any adverse changes. If such arise, then typical provisions will entitle the customer either to seek additional comfort from the service provider, such as a parent company guarantee if not already provided, or to exit the agreement.

3.   **The service provider perspective**
Similar to the customer perspective, from the service provider perspective, due diligence again covers two concepts:
- the due diligence that the service provider will perform; and
- the service provider's attitude to due diligence as encapsulated by the terms of the contract.

3.1   **The due diligence the service provider will perform**
In a typical outsource project (for example), a service provider will provide the customer with an extensive due diligence request list, then follow up with a multitude of supplemental requests as it examines the customer's technical and operational requirements. The same approach would likely be followed for other technology projects where due diligence is required.

From the service provider perspective this is essential so that the service provider can properly price the required services as well as check that it is capable of providing all of the required services. In addition the due diligence undertaken by the service provider will often unearth issues with the existing service provision, be that as provided by the incumbent or by the customer itself. That detective work will be invaluable from the service provider perspective because it will lead directly into the contract clauses that the service provider is willing to accept, both in terms of risk transfer and in terms of ability to meet expected service levels.

The list of elements which the service provider will explore is essentially the mirror of the list above for the customer but seen from a different perspective. The service provider must uncover the following.

- *Service boundary*. Where does the service provider obligation to provide services start and finish? The service provider will need to ensure that the scope of services is clear, and set, and to avoid unexpected elements which might be implied into the service provision, but which had not been priced.

- *Technology requirements*. The service provider must ask itself whether it will need to take-on existing technology, and wind that down over its life, or replace it with its own solution. If the service provider is taking on existing technology it will need to examine the terms and conditions on which that is currently provided and make an assessment as to whether it can rely on such new sub-contractors.

- *Issues with current services*. Are the current users unhappy? Have there been outages and incidents which the service provider is being asked to fix? Are those incidents purely technology related or might there have been 'people issues' associated too? It will be key for the service provider to dig into this point to ensure that its own solution, while being a theoretically brilliant solution, is not doomed to failure because of the user attitudes and 'tissue rejection' of the processes themselves.

- *The people*. Who is currently providing the service? Are they experts with essential knowledge that the service provider must speak to, and indeed can the service provider take them into its team through a Transfer of Undertakings (Protection of Employment) Regulations 2006 (TUPE) transfer? One of the most key elements of any due diligence from the service provider perspective is the human capital element. This will inform not only the solution that the service provider is able to offer but also the basis for the price offered, having factored in the cost of the transfer and the terms and conditions of the affected workforce. As detailed in Chapter 14, the service provider will need to know details of the terms and conditions of all potentially relevant staff, and also details of their wider employment status; including any claims, disciplinary issues and sickness so that it can assess fully the worth, and cost, of the transferring team. TUPE at Regulation 11 requires the outsourcing customer to pass relevant staff details to the incoming service provider 28 days before the transfer. This will be too late for a due diligence exercise but of course the General Data Protection Regulation (GDPR) only allows processing of personal data if one of the conditions in Article 6 is met. As such a balance needs to be struck and the service provider should request that the customer anonymise the staff information if it is to be disclosed as part of a due diligence exercise earlier than the 28-day period.

3.2   Service provider attitude to typical contractual clauses

(a)   Risk transfer

A typical customer clause regarding due diligence will seek to transfer the risk of due diligence to the service provider. Put simply, the clause will be a statement that the service provider "has exhausted all necessary due diligence, has satisfied itself, and has entered into the agreement fully informed". It will often then go on to say that "anything subsequently discovered will be at the service provider's own risk". This is clearly problematic from the service provider's perspective; how can the service provider be completely sure that it has unearthed everything it needs to know? As such the service provider will need to qualify such a provision; either through a knowledge qualification (ie, wording to the effect of "so far as the service provider is aware..."), or by retaining the right to revisit obligations and charges in the event that information is wrong, or new facts come to light.

As such a post-contract variation right is essential from the service provider's perspective. One particular variation right arises in relation to the service level regime.

(b)   Service levels

The service provider will be asked at execution of contract to commit to meeting, or exceeding service levels. There will often be an attendant penalty for failure in the form of service credits. From the service provider perspective this can adversely impact the expected profit margin from the deal. To protect that profit margin the service provider needs to know that the service levels are (easily) achievable. So where those service levels have been based on previous performance by a third-party incumbent or indeed by the customer itself, it is essential for the service provider to negotiate a 'bedding-in period' whereby the service levels are measured, but do not lead to any penalty. Instead there needs to be a mechanism for recalibration as the nature of the service and the surrounding factors that affect that service become better understood. This is a form of post-contract variation through real-life monitoring which can help to protect the service provider from finding itself locked into a bad deal.

(c)   *Contractualising assumptions and dependencies*
A service provider's ability to agree to a risk/reward profile, balancing required services, service levels, expected revenue and profit and potential liability risk will be informed by the outputs of its due diligence exercise, and the extent to which it is able to couch its proposition in terms of assumptions and dependencies. A service provider should be keen to play-back to a customer the basis upon which it has calculated its price and its expectations of the customer. It is not uncommon for a contract to feature some form of Risks, Assumptions, Issues and Dependencies (RAID) log to make it clear who is responsible for what. This will allow the service provider to avoid unnecessary blame and liability where it has been prevented from performing because of an earlier failure by the customer.

4.   Potential solutions

4.1   Suitable period for due diligence
It is clear that a properly run due diligence exercise is costly and time consuming for both parties. But cut short, the risks of misaligned expectations are apparent. In a competitive RfP scenario the issue is magnified: service providers will be reluctant to spend too much time where their chances of securing the contract are slim because due diligence may end up as an unrecoverable bid cost. Equally, customers will not want to spend time being interviewed by, and providing endless information to, a stream of potential providers.

Pragmatism is the order of the day. A tightly run due diligence exercise, controlled centrally and run by the customer through a data room allowing bilateral access for each bidder is the solution. The customer must take the time and make the effort to make the information as accurate and exhaustive as possible (so that the customer can stand behind the veracity of the information). The service provider must accept the bid cost of extensive due diligence so that it can price accurately and have confidence in its ability to provide the required services, particularly where a customer is seeking a transformative solution. There have been situations where a customer has been too secretive and then wondered why the bids received are unaffordable.

4.2 Blanket of confidentiality

To make the process as smooth as possible and to protect the commercial interests of both parties it is sensible to put a non-disclosure agreement in place. A customer may, if running a competitive tender, have already established principles of confidentiality as they apply to the bid process. That will allow the service provider to be privy to sensitive information. While there may be some information that the customer would rather not disclose, this can be a false economy; leaving the service provider to guess will inevitably mean that a risk premium is ascribed to areas of uncertainty, making the solution more expensive. The flip side is also true; if the customer is seeking to select a service provider on the basis of lowest price, then that will have the unintended consequence of incentivising the service provider to not include a risk premium for unknown factors; instead meaning that the seemingly low-price bid will be cast in terms of assumptions and dependencies.

4.3 Typical due diligence clause and bounded right to post-contract variation

Once the due diligence has been completed, and the terms and conditions of the outsourcing agreement are being finalised, both parties will want to record the basis on which they have entered into the agreement.

A middle-path due diligence clause should feature the following concepts:

- an acknowledgment that the service provider has performed its own due diligence, and entered into the agreement with its eyes open, and not in reliance on statements made by the customer (this is pro-customer);
- a statement that the above non-reliance acknowledgment is without prejudice to any specific conditions set out in the agreement (as to, for example, quality and suitability of transferring assets) (this is balanced);

- an ability for the service provider to raise flags where information is inaccurate or incomplete (this is pro-service provider);
- a process to deal with those flags whereby the parties agree whether the inaccuracies or incompleteness is material, and if so, allowing for a change to be made through the agreement change control procedure (this is balanced/pro-service provider); and
- a check and balance to the automatic change process above whereby the materiality of the inaccuracy or incompleteness is assessed in terms of good industry practice that should be assumed of a sensible service provider performing due diligence (this is pro-customer).

4.4   Relief event mechanism

Where the parties have agreed that the agreement will list out assumptions and dependencies, then the consequences of those assumptions being proven wrong, or the dependencies not being performed, must be addressed. Typically a relief event clause will feature in one form or another. A service provider will seek to be relieved of its obligation to perform where it could not perform because of an act of omission of the customer. For example, if a service provider has not met a required service level because of a customer failing, then it may be that the parties agree that the service provider is 'deemed' to have met that level (ie, service credits will not accrue).

From the customer perspective it will be inevitable that the service provider's proposition be couched in terms of certain assumptions and dependencies, but the customer can minimise these through detailed discussion, and through a relief event mechanism which puts the onus on the service provider to make the case that relief is justified. A tougher clause will say that the service provider will lose its right (be estopped) and be prevented from seeking relief if that application is not made promptly, and within a specified period (say, six months).

Summing up, what seems a dry and procedural part of deal conclusion is actually a fundamental part of the overall negotiation process, both for service provider and customer. As stated above, the courts will not seek to rewrite a bad deal it its terms are clear. As such it is essential that both parties do all that they can to be clear on the basis of their deal. Complex outsourcings and transformational deals merely amplify this need and the consequences of failing to take the due diligence exercise seriously are clear. It is not the case that the customer can merely insert a tough due diligence clause and fold its arms. It is for the customer to ensure that the service provider has understood the requirements and all relevant context otherwise it will be cold comfort for a customer to have a robust clause, but a failed project.

2. Service provisions

1. Introduction

It may be tempting to think that the detailing of the parts of a sourcing or outsourcing contract which sets out the actual services to be provided will be relatively straightforward, albeit potentially time consuming. After all, the customer knows what it wants to receive/buy and the service provider knows what it wants to provide/sell, or so it is believed.

The reality, however, is more complex. Many forms of technology procurement (and in particular the large-scale, more complex engagements such as outsourcing projects) can involve extremely detailed and nuanced sets of requirements, with the potential for different interpretations as between customer and service provider. What the service provider is offering to provide may also not be a perfect match to what the customer had originally asked for, such that one party or the other may have a decision to make as to whether it is willing to change/compromise (and to what extent). Trying to predict all of these potential grey areas in advance can be extremely difficult, but is nonetheless of great importance to both parties, as we will explain below.

There is, accordingly, no getting around the need to invest significant effort into the description of what is actually to be undertaken by way of service provision (and the associated deliverables/work products, dependencies upon the other parties etc). However, in this chapter we will consider the various other components of the process of contract drafting which relate to the service description, and the interests of the parties in relation to them.

2. The customer perspective

2.1 The services description

The relevant contract will need to contain a section which describes what it is that the customer expects to receive by way of the relevant services. In many cases this will be bespoke and specific to the customer (eg, if the customer is seeking a solution which is unique to its particular circumstances). In others, it will be very detailed but may nonetheless have a commodity element to it (eg, in relation to certain kinds of IT outsourcing services, where the description of the operation of a particular facet of the services – such as the functioning of a service desk or the provision of desk-side support – may be capable of standardisation). Where the customer is procuring more generic or 'off the shelf' services or products (including many forms of software as a service (SaaS) offering), however, it may expect to start from the standard service descriptions provided by the service provider, but may still want to review and amend them, so as to ensure that they are adequately detailed and do not contain too many ambiguities or overtly service provider-friendly provisions.

This will usually be a time-consuming process, and while the customer's legal/contract advisers will play an important role in terms of contract drafting and identifying potential areas of concern or doubt which should be addressed, the primary responsibility in this regard will fall upon the customer's subject matter experts (who will both know the detail of what it is that the customer needs, and also be best placed to identify whether what the service provider is setting out in the contractual service description is a good fit with those requirements, and/or is sufficiently clear).

2.2 Linkage to request for proposal

If the contract in question has been entered into pursuant to some form of formal procurement process (eg, whereby the customer sent out an initial request for proposal (RfP) to describe its requirements, and the service provider responded to it in order to confirm both its willingness and ability to provide the required services).

In the ideal world, therefore, the customer may seek to include a commitment in the contract that the service provider will provide a solution or set of services which will meet the requirements set out in such RfP documentation, such that any other service related details which are contained in the contract become more of an explanation as to how the service provider proposes to meet the customer's requirements, rather than a limitation as to what those requirements actually are. In order to achieve this, the customer may seek to have the RfP documentation made as part of the contract (either by including it in the contract documentation and/or by incorporating it by reference), and by providing that it will take precedence over any conflicting provisions elsewhere in the contract documentation.

2.3 Implied services

Notwithstanding the amount of effort that may be invested in getting the service descriptions drafted to a level of detail and completeness that is as good as is reasonably possible, there remains the possibility for dispute and ambiguity. The more complex and widely scoped the project is, the greater the risk. For example, this is the case in the context of technology outsourcing agreements (which do not have the same certainty of scope as would be the case with a form of deliverable-based contract, where the scope of responsibilities is more inextricably linked with the acceptance criteria for the associated deliverables).

For outsource style contracts in particular, therefore, the customer will likely press for the inclusion of what is often referred to as a 'sweep' clause, that is, a provision which reflects the fact that notwithstanding the best efforts of both parties, there remains the risk that some elements of the service descriptions will remain inadequate and will miss elements which – on a good faith/objective basis – should have been included. The objective of the customer in this regard is to avoid the risk of what is sometimes described as 'death by change control'. This is the situation whereby the customer thinks that there is agreement as to the scope of the services which it is to receive, but after the contract is signed – and when the bargaining leverage of the customer is much reduced – the service provider starts to take a more literal view of the wording in the relevant services description and claim a right to be paid extra amounts of money whenever the customer asks for anything which is not exactly described within it.

The customer's interests would obviously be best served by having such a 'sweep' clause drafted as widely as possible. This will depend somewhat upon the nature of the actual project in question, but drafting options for the customer to consider will include:

- those services, tasks and activities which would be 'reasonably, ordinarily, inherently or customarily' implied or considered to be a normal part of the scope of services of the nature or type of the services as required by the agreement, or which are necessary to them;
- those activities which would ordinarily be undertaken by any personnel who actually transfer to the service provider pursuant to the agreement in question (eg, as a result of the operation of The Transfer of Undertakings (Protection of

Employment) Regulations 2006 (TUPE)/the Acquired Rights Directive (ARD));

- the services which were previously undertaken/provided pursuant to third-party contracts which are assigned or novated to the service provider in connection with the agreement;
- services which were previously provided, but which are then displaced by the agreement with the service provider; and
- activities previously undertaken pursuant to any internal budget which is pertinent to the activities now to be undertaken by the service provider, as part of the business case for the project in question.

The customer will want to specify that all such tasks will be considered to be part of the core services, such that there is no question of the application of any change control process, nor any additional charges to be levied by the service provider in return for the completion of such aspects of the services.

The requirement for such a clause is less pressing where the nature of the contract is fundamentally focused upon the production of specific work products/deliverables; in such cases, the focus of the customer will be more on ensuring that the acceptance criteria relevant to such deliverables (and the process for the acceptance tests in relation to them) are fully addressed in the contract.

2.4   Customer dependencies

Ideally, the customer may wish the relevant services to be totally within the control of the service provider, such that the ability of the service provider to meet its obligations is not limited by or contingent upon any particular inputs or responsibilities of the customer itself. This may indeed be the case in some instances, but there will often be at least some things that the customer will need to do in order to facilitate the provision of the services.

The interest of the customer in this regard will be to:

- ensure that such obligations are set out on an exhaustive basis (eg, with no doubt as to whether there are other obligations which have yet to be set out);
- see that the obligations are set out in an unambiguous and adequately clear manner, and are not unnecessarily wide or onerous; and
- require that if it is contended that the customer has not met any of its own obligations, this is promptly notified in

accordance with the agreement's relevant requirements (see Chapter 7 regarding relief/excused events).

2.5 Acceptance and approvals

As noted above, where the nature of the contract is predicated upon the completion and delivery of particular work products as opposed for the ongoing provision of specific services, the customer will be particularly focused upon the acceptance and approvals process.

The key aspects that the customer will want to see covered off in this regard will include:

- the inclusion of the detailed acceptance criteria in the agreement, or else a clear process by which such acceptance criteria will be agreed (by express cross reference to the requirements of the agreement); and
- the process for acceptance testing, which would include:
  - a commitment by the service provider to assist with the testing process;
  - an obligation upon the service provider to promptly correct any identified deficiencies (and ideally within a pre-set time frame), and without additional charge to the customer; and
  - a 'long stop' date by which all identified deficiencies or nonconformities must have been addressed, failing which the customer would be entitled to terminate the contract (by reason of breach).

Even if the contract is more focused upon ongoing services, there will remain the need for the customer to specify how certain key milestones will be determined to have been successfully achieved. For example, in the context of a cloud services deal, a key question may be: has the cloud service successfully commenced, with connectivity established to a solution configured in line with customer's expectations? In relation to an outsourcing transaction, the completion of the initial transition activities will obviously need to have criteria attached to it so as to establish successful completion, but there may also be subsequent transformational activities which will also need to be tested/confirmed to have been successfully completed.

2.6 Warranty/post go-live

Even after acceptance/approvals have been provided, there remains the risk that problems will arise. If the contract is for ongoing service obligations, then this will likely be adequately addressed by the service provider's service level commitments and/or obligations to provide the services in line with the relevant service descriptions, but if the agreement is one for more one-off delivery, the customer will want to ensure that the service provider is obliged to correct any such problems promptly and without additional charge to the customer.

3.   The service provider perspective

3.1   The services description

The service provider's overriding concern is for certainty, namely that it will fully understand what it is to deliver, such that it can adequately and completely assess its costs to be incurred in doing so.

In this regard, the service provider will push for the services description to be a complete and inclusive list of its service delivery obligations. Where its offering is based on a more standardised or commodity style proposition (eg, the delivery of a cloud-based service), it may actually be insistent that the service description be based upon its own standard service description/documentation, on the basis that this is not amenable to customer-specific modification.

3.2   Linkage to request for proposal

The service provider view in this regard may well be that while the customer's RfP will have set out what the customer wanted to receive; this is not the same as representing what the service provider then stated that it was willing to provide. So, while the customer may have asked for [ABCD], the service provider's proposition in response may have been to offer [BCDE]. In such circumstances, the service provider will say that it cannot then be said to be obliged to provide [A], as that was never part of what the service provider had proposed.

In any event, the service provider will likely argue that the RfP will be subject to extensive commercial discussion, not just in terms of formal responses but also during potential workshops, email exchanges, discussions etc. As such, it would be very difficult to track all of the variations/clarifications which have been understood by the parties as being a precursor to the contract, and therefore both safer and more certain to simply rely upon what is explicitly agreed in the detailed services description, rather than harking back to any more historic RfP documentation.

3.3 Implied services

The strong preference for the service provider will be to avoid any kind of 'sweep' provisions in their entirety, and to instead point solely to the agreed service description as contained within (or incorporated by reference in) the actual agreement. As noted above, where the service provider is proposing a solution which is predicated upon its own service delivery model, it may insist upon the starting point being its own form of drafting, rather than any form of drafting proposed by the customer (and indeed may in some cases insist on this being largely unamended, eg, in relation to commodity style software or cloud-based services which are not amenable to amendment or adjustment). The service provider will thus argue that if anything is missed in the service description, it will necessarily be out of scope and therefore be subject to the change control process.

3.4 Customer dependencies

The service provider will want to safeguard itself against the risk that the customer will not pull its weight in terms of the delivery of the services. The nature of the delivery of technology-based services is that they will often necessitate some degree of change in terms of what the customer and its employees have been doing before, and/or may necessitate the customer undertaking specific actions or investments so as to facilitate the successful completion of the service provider's responsibilities.

While the service provider will likely have no problem in having as many of these obligations specifically set out as is possible (on the basis that this creates certainty), it will be wary about this being seen as an inclusive list, as it is difficult to predict up front quite what the position may be 'on the ground' within the customer's organisation. Accordingly, the service provider may push for the inclusion of some more generic customer obligations to provide all such support, advice, information and decision making as may reasonably be required by the service provider.

3.5 Acceptance and approvals

Having a clear cut-off in terms of acceptance and approvals is as much in the service provider's interests as it is for the customer, not least because this will often be linked with other provisions in the contract such as the commencement of warranty periods, and the triggering of payment obligations.

In such regard, however, the service provider will want to ensure that:

- any acceptance criteria are mutually agreed, and expressly linked back to the actual requirements of the agreement (as opposed to more subjective requirements of the customer or its personnel);
- the customer itself devotes sufficient time and resource to the testing process, and completes it within an agreed time frame (such that the service provider is not left hanging, without knowing whether the customer is satisfied with its work or not);
- it has a reasonable period of time to complete any necessary adjustments/rework; and
- the customer will not in any event unreasonably withhold or delay its confirmation of acceptance or approval.

3.6 Warranty/post go-live

Depending on the nature of the services or products being provided, the service provider may:

- subsume the outputs into the core 'business as usual' services (such that if any issues arise with any aspects of the services, they are addressed as part of the ongoing service arrangements, eg, as part of any wider service level related arrangements, or a separate support services commitment);
- provide a limited warranty (eg, whereby – for a limited period such as 90 days – the service provider will commit to correct any identified failures to comply with the agreed contract requirements); and/or
- see the confirmation of acceptance/approval as a 'cut-off' point, for example, such that the customer's acceptance or approval is in effect a binding confirmation that the service provider has completed all that was required of it in connection with the services/work products in question.

4. Potential solutions

4.1 The services description

The solution to this issue will certainly depend on the nature of the project and service offering in question. If, for example, the service provider is providing a standard SaaS solution, there can be little if any question of a 'sweep' clause and instead the focus will be on whether the customer has adequately assessed what the service provider's standard service documentation provides for.

If the services in question are of more of an ongoing nature (eg, managed services or outsourcing), then the options for compromise may include:

- limiting the inclusion of any implied services to those which can be proactively identified during a specified and limited period (eg, during a transition period or a set number of months thereafter); and/or
- applying a cost related limitation to the inclusion of implied services (on the basis that if the services argued to fall within such a provision exceed such a cost threshold, then the parties might fairly be said to have proceeded on the basis of a mutual mistake as to what is involved with the project).

4.2 Linkage to request for proposal

The inclusion of the RfP documents for a project is often problematic, given that such documentation is often drafted on an aspirational basis.

However, such documents nonetheless represent that intention of the customer, and, accordingly, a potential compromise may be to recognise that while the agreement is ultimately the core determinant of what the agreement to the parties shall be (including as to the scope of the services), the customer's RfP shall nonetheless be given contractual significance by way of being used as the determinant for the purposes of resolving any acknowledged ambiguities or debates as to interpretation. This may in some cases be given additional 'teeth' by linking it to independent third-party expert determination.

4.3 Implied services

For continuing/outsourced services at least, it may be entirely market standard to have some level of 'sweep' provisions, but this will not normally extend to services which are simply ancillary to the services or necessary to their delivery, as that may extend the scope beyond what the parties may reasonably have intended.

As noted above regarding the scope of the services description, the implied services language will be capable of limitation both as to duration of the period during which any additional requirements must be notified, and the costs associated with their provision.

Such provisions may be less relevant (and capable, therefore, of being omitted) for more discrete delivery-orientated technology contracts, where the focus will instead be on the detail of the specification of what the service provider has to deliver.

4.4 Customer dependencies

Customers will only rarely agree to broadly crafted 'catch all' dependencies or requirements, although some at least may be justified (eg, a requirement to provide reasonable office facilities to service provider personnel who may be based onshore/working at the customer's facilities).

4.5 Acceptance and approvals

In order to create a practical incentive for the customer to get on to complete acceptance/approvals within the anticipated timeframes and so as not to impact negatively upon the overall project timeframes, it may be possible to agree a deemed acceptance process, that is, whereby the customer is given appropriate notice of the need to accept or approve relevant services or deliverables, has all that it needs to do so, and yet then fails to do so. In such circumstances, the customer may then be deemed to have accepted the relevant services or deliverables (so as to enable it to invoice for any related payment milestones, and also to be entitled to charge the customer for any subsequent rework to any such accepted services or deliverables as may be required in the future). The customer will in this regard wish to ensure that it has been provided with adequate knowledge and notice of the acceptance/approval process, and all necessary support from the service provider itself. The customer will likely also want to provide that while deemed acceptance will trigger payment etc, it will not constitute a waiver of the customer's rights or remedies regarding any actual deficiencies in the service provider's deliverables or services, as may subsequently be identified.

4.6 Warranty/post go-live

There is an obvious potential overlap between the scope of post-delivery warranty services, and any subsequent business as usual (BAU) services or support services. Accordingly, the focus of the post go-live warranty service is largely relevant to those technology services which are primarily delivery orientated.

In such cases, a potential compromise may be to state that the primary liability of the service provider will be to come back and correct any identified non-conformities with the requirements of the agreement. However, if the service provider fails to do so, then the potential compromise may be to provide that the customer shall then retain its rights to claim damages/contract remedies (eg, contract termination, in worse case).

3. Compliance with laws and regulations

1. Introduction

It is a basic and fundamentally straightforward and true statement that a party to a contract should comply with laws and regulations and should be able to commit that to the other party. After all, this is a commitment that a party makes by coming into existence (no one separately contractually agrees with the government, law enforcement agencies or regulators to comply with laws) and it is a fair and reasonable expectation that a party should only do business with a party that is complying with laws and regulations.

While this seems like a fairly anodyne statement, the truth is slightly different in technology and outsourcing contracts. While parties of course accept that they have to comply with laws, they debate whether they need to make that commitment to a third party, in addition to the relevant enforcement agencies. There is also often a significant argument over what laws ought to be complied with, and in respect of what and at what time. There is even a debate over what a law is, and the extent to which it should include codes of practice and guidelines issued by regulators.

In longer-term service agreements, the compliance with law obligations can be (and often should be) one of most complicated and debated terms of the agreement, as they drive scope, risk and commercial issues.

2. The customer perspective

A customer will want its suppliers to comply with laws and provide a set of services and outputs that are compliant with laws and regulations. The reason for this is not so much to shift compliance risk but because it will need a supplier to contribute to its overall compliance approach and activities and will want to have its suppliers provide inputs that match and meet the customer's overall compliance framework requirements.

If the service provider does not, or the outputs of the services do not, comply with laws and regulations, the inherent value of the outputs is reduced, from the customer perspective. This is because, without this commitment, the customer cannot be sure that its use of them will be lawful, let alone will allow it to meet its own responsibilities, and the customer would need to rework the outputs at additional cost and effort to make them a viable output.

It is of course important to note that regulated entities cannot outsource their own compliance and regulatory responsibilities to the relevant regulators so it can never be the case that the terms of a sourcing/technology contract can be taken by a customer to achieve its regulatory responsibilities.

2.1   What is a law for the purposes of this commitment?

The definition of law or applicable law around which the obligation gravitates should be as broadly cast as possible, to capture any legal or regulatory obligation that might be relevant (the meaning of relevance or applicable is discussed below).

In this regard, then, it would capture laws issued by governments, regulations issued by regulators and any guidelines, guidance or similar issued by governments or regulators. Guidance and codes of practice are important inclusions as these are the clear and obvious way to interpret the laws/regulations and, as they are issued by these bodies, are effectively the same as 'genuine' laws even if they are positioned as guidance. The definition should of course capture the relevant civil code or common law, as relevant, although we have had one counter-party argue that common law (ie, court judgments) should not be included as they were capable of appeal and change such that the service provider's obligation was not clear, notwithstanding that this perspective undermines a fundamental tenet of English law going back over 1,000 years.

Once the basic understanding of a law is established (and going forward, we refer to law in this section as being all of the broader definition), the debate turns to which laws are applicable. For example, is it appropriate for the service provider to commit to a customer that it should comply with laws – and be open to a breach of contract claim – in respect of laws that are wholly irrelevant to the subject matter of the agreement? The answer is: probably not, and this is often easily fixed by referring to a requirement to comply with applicable laws.

From a customer's point of view, there would be little distinction drawn with regards to which party the laws apply; the customer will want the service provider to commit to adhering to laws that are applicable, and this means applicable to the agreement and the services to be provided pursuant to its terms, not just applicable to a particular entity.

As discussed below, there is often a debate over whether the customer ought to inform the supplier over the laws that apply to the customer or the customer's sector.

2.2 Who should commit to comply with laws?

Clearly, the customer's preference will be that the service provider should make a promise to comply with applicable laws. The customer will want to be assured that it is doing business with an entity that is adhering to applicable laws, both in terms of contracting with appropriate entities, to provide it with some comfort from a compliance (eg, human rights in the supply chain, anti-bribery etc) point of view and also in order to support the customer's own compliance commitments, especially where the customer itself is in a regulated sector.

The customer will often resist any suggested imposition of a reciprocal obligation made to the service provider with respect to the customer also being required to comply with laws. This is positioned on a number of bases. First, the customer is not providing services to the service provider and so it does not need to adhere to the same standards. Such a commitment is simply irrelevant in the context of the relationship envisaged by the agreement. Secondly, the customer does not need to commit to comply with laws to a service provider. If the customer does not comply, the service provider will not be exposed because the customer's non-compliance will not affect the service provider. It will be a matter for the relevant law enforcement agencies/regulators. Thirdly, the customer is not set up to commit to comply with laws with regards to this kind of relationship. While in some sectors, of course, the customer's commitment to its own end clients is paramount and its compliance focus will be in that direction, and not towards its supply chain.

2.3 What should be delivered and provided in accordance with laws?

The customer will expect the service provider to perform all its obligations in accordance with applicable laws, and especially that it comply with laws, and the services and the outputs of the services will be delivered in accordance with and themselves comply with applicable laws.

It is important, from a customer point of view, to ensure that both the manner of delivery and the scope of the services are compliant with laws. This reference to both aspects means that the delivery model will need to be compliant, which could be important in relation to, for example, security methods, or the set-up of the service provider's operation. Whereas the reference to the scope is important to ensure that the customer is receiving a set of compliant services, for example, making sure that finance and accounting services relating to keeping accounts adhere to relevant accounting standards and regulations.

As to outputs or deliverables of the services, the customer will want to ensure that these also adhere to relevant legal standards so that they can be used with confidence and, again, support the customer's broader compliance responsibilities. Realistically, a customer might need to recognise some degree of time limitation on the duration of such commitment and, likely, some scope limitations (that is the output will be compliant for a particular purpose, but not for others).

2.4   Which jurisdiction's laws are being referred to?

While an agreement will contain a governing law, this would not be intended to determine the laws to which the compliance with laws obligations relate. The customer expectation will be that the service provider should be skilled and experienced enough to form a view as to which laws would need to be covered off, and that the customer can expect the broadest promise on the basis the service provider takes the responsibility for the analysis of the relevant laws to be applied and adhered to.

If the customer were to agree any limitations as to the geographical scope of applicable laws, it would be keen to ensure that the relevant laws should at the very least cover both the countries from which the services were provided and also in respect of which the services are to be provided. This would then cover the locations in which the service provider was located and so provide some comfort that the service provider was operating in a legally compliant fashion, whist the reference to the countries in respect of which the services were to be received would relate to the scope of the services themselves, looking at the requirement from the perspective of the customer's needs.

If the customer is minded to agree to any such geographical limits, it ought to consider the basis on which the services will be provided and accessed. For example, access to services on a remote access basis or via a distributed network needs to be more carefully considered to make sure that the services are being legally provided via these means and in respect of all the relevant countries.

2.5   What happens if there is a change in law?

On the basis that the customer expects the service provider to commit to supplying the services and providing the outputs, and otherwise performing its obligation in applicable law, if there is a change to law then this will need to be taken into account by the service provider and it will need to make such changes that are required in order to meet this primary contractual obligation.

Many customers will want to have some degree of input into the manner in which the change will be implemented and how it will affect the scope of the services being delivered to it. As such, the change ought to be governed by the change control procedure, so that the customer can influence and control the scope of changes. The challenge for the service provider in this regard will be whether the changes that the customer wants to see exceed those it was prepared to make or feels able to make with regards to its broader client base. Making such special changes might also then cause the service provider to incur costs specific to the customer's requirements that it otherwise would not have had to incur. Consequently, while a customer might expect that the responsibility to achieve ongoing compliance with laws is effectively part and parcel of the service provider's running costs that therefore don't concern the customer, it is relatively normal for a customer to accept that if it has incremental requirements over and above the changes required to maintain a 'base' level of consistency with the legal requirements, it will need to bear these costs relating to such incremental requirements.

3.   The service provider perspective

Service providers will often approach compliance with law from the perspective of it not being an overarching fundamental requirement in itself, but instead as forming part of the requirements with which it would need to comply, simply like any other service requirement. So, taking this point of view, it logically makes sense that it is the customer's responsibility to be clear about the relevant laws, and moreover as to how the services need to be delivered in order to achieve compliance with the laws. That is, if something needs to be done to achieve compliance with a particular law, it needs to be set out plainly in the agreement in the same way that one would set out the tasks making up a service description.

3.1   What is a law for the purposes of this commitment?

From the viewpoint of the service provider, what falls within the scope of 'laws' should be clear, binding and definitive. References to guidance or codes of practice do not have legal effect and so should not be treated as laws, because compliance with them would create a broader burden than is actually required, and could result in the service provider adhering to the wrong set of principles in connection with the terms of the agreement and, more broadly, exposing itself to its own compliance issues.

So, a service provider will likely prefer a much narrower definition of laws so as to remove the codes of practice and, potentially, even some regulatory requirements.

Additionally, the service provider will look to ensure that applicable laws means those that apply to it as a business. These are the laws with which it is required to comply as part of being a going concern. Other laws that might, for example, relate to the scope of the services or to the customer, fall more within the category of being a set of deal-specific requirements. As such these ought not be part of the basic compliance obligation on the part of the service provider, but only a service provider responsibility insofar as they are articulated to form part of a services description.

3.2 Who should commit to comply with laws?

The service provider might well expect that, just as the customer has an expectation that it is doing business with an entity that is compliant with laws, the service provider has a similar expectation. It would then anticipate that the customer would comply with applicable laws and would commit to this via a contractual obligation. This would be relevant not just from a compliance perspective, but also in terms of being, effectively, a service dependency. That is, if the customer was not compliant with laws, the service provider would not be at fault for failing to provide the services as a consequence. In the context of data protection, for example, the service provider may argue that it would itself be more exposed to potential claims if the customer has not complied with its own obligations as to the gathering of personal data and the confirmation of the purposes for which it can be processed.

3.3 What should be delivered and provided in accordance with laws?

The service provider will likely agree that it would provide the services and perform the agreement in accordance with applicable laws, insofar as these applicable laws are those that relate to it as a going concern. As above, if there are any customer-specific laws or laws relevant to the services, these would need to be spelled out in the service description. Many service providers will take a slightly more pragmatic approach to this latter aspect where the service itself is intrinsically linked to a series of compliance activities. For example, in certain countries it is not permissible to take certain accounting records outside of that country. Service providers who regularly provide the finance and accounting services should be aware of these constraints and should have set up the service in order to comply with these inherent requirements and constraints, such that these would not need to be set out in the services description or elsewhere in the agreement. However, many will still argue that such obligations should nonetheless still be set out in the actual service description (especially if the customer has any specific nuances as to how it has worked in the past, or operates in unfamiliar jurisdictions).

3.4 **Which jurisdiction's laws are being referred to?**
The perspective on this will of course depend on which laws are in scope of the initial compliance responsibility. Assuming it is those that relate to the service provider only as a going concern, this would likely lead to an expectation that it is any laws that impact the service provider. If the obligation has broadened to cover other laws, the service provider will be concerned about the compliance risk and financial consequences of having to carry out a detailed assessment of all these laws. Multi-jurisdictional compliance programmes tend to be expensive and need to be kept up to date. Service providers will often argue that given they are not legal service providers, they cannot bear this responsibility.

3.5 **What happens if there is a change in law?**
Based on the premise that the service provider complies with laws applicable to it, it will be responsible for ensuring ongoing compliance with these laws, including as they are changed. For other laws, the customer will need to be responsible for informing the service provider via a change control process of the impacts on the services, and how these services and other requirements of the agreement need to be changed to reflect the new or different laws.

4. **Potential compromises**
The parties to technology contracts will frequently be able to find some middle ground in connection with the negotiated position on compliance with provisions of laws. Each deal is of course unique, and the end position tends to be more in favour of the customer,

particularly in business process outsourcings where the nature of the services to be performed is especially linked to regulatory compliance, whether that is in relation to finance and accounting, linked to accounting rules or settlement, or post trade subject to industry and market standards. The position may, however, be more service-provider centric regarding more commodity style services, where the service provider may stick to its guns in arguing that it is generally for the customer to then confirm whether the service on offer will meet its legal requirements.

4.1   What is a law for the purposes of this commitment?
The scope of the relevant definition will likely be determined by what is actually binding because it is a genuine law or regulation, together with those codes of practice that adherence to a good industry practice standard would dictate should be complied with. If it is good industry practice to comply with guidance or codes of practice, these are effectively akin to laws on the basis that the relevant regulator will except such compliance and would take (non-)compliance into account when assessing the performance of the customer/service provider.

In terms of a split between 'supplier laws' and 'customer laws', it is not unusual to see that parties agree to differentiate between these two in the following ways.

- 'Customer laws' are defined as being laws applicable to the customer only by virtue of and in its capacity of being engaged in certain business activities (eg, because the customer is a pharmaceutical company, it is subject to specific requirements that otherwise would not be applicable). By contrast, 'supplier laws' would be any laws that are not customer laws, and this would include laws relevant to the service provider as a going concern, and also to the basic scope of the services and the manner of providing the services, as well as generic laws which apply to the world at large.
- It becomes the customer's responsibility to inform the service provider of the customer laws that are relevant to the arrangements/scope envisaged by the agreement, and once informed the service provider must provide the agreement, including the services in accordance with the notified customer laws. This is an ongoing responsibility on the customer, and so the customer retains the obligation to inform the service provider of changes to these 'customer laws' as they occur.

Accordingly, the service provider then retains responsibility to ensure compliance with and bear the costs in connection with changes to the service provider. There is often a debate as to the extent to which the service provider should bear the total liability for the costs involved in making changes to the services to ensure consistency with applicable laws. This is explored below.

Note that it is also possible to have an even more granular split, if 'supplier laws' are further divided between those laws specific to service providers; the laws which are specific to the type of services being provided; and generic laws.

4.2   Who should commit to comply with laws?

Once the split between customer laws and suppler laws is settled, the compliance with laws issues tend to become easier to resolve. The service provider's responsibility is more straightforward. However, it is worth considering carefully whether the service provider itself needs to comply with the customer laws or whether it needs to provide the services and the outputs of the services in accordance with the relevant laws.

Likewise, whether a customer ought to agree to comply with laws will depend on the specifics of a given situation. For example, it might not need to agree with laws which simply do not affect the relationship as between the parties or which are owed more directly to a supervisory third party such as a regulator. It might, however, agree to comply with laws that do more immediately go to the heart of the relationship between the parties, such as data protection compliance. These kinds of commitments can therefore be assessed and given on a more specific rather than generic basis.

4.3   What should be delivered and provided in accordance with applicable laws?

It is of course important that the services and the outputs of the services are provided in accordance with the applicable laws. A continuing point of debate will be whether the service provider is responsible for working out how the services and the deliverables ought to take into account the customer laws (assuming the customer has the responsibility to actually inform the service provider of the laws) or whether the customer should be responsible for articulating in the agreement how the services need to be delivered so as to meet the requirements (and any changes to them). The parties must accordingly agree not only who has to monitor the laws, but also who has to interpret them.

One issue for the parties to further consider will be continuing compliance. For example, should compliance be measured at a point in time (eg, delivery)? Or, should there be an ongoing responsibility, particularly with regards to outputs, in respect of which an ongoing compliance responsibility is more likely to be the case where the service provider is providing a managed service or outsourced services (or potentially where updates to ensure compliance form part of a support and maintenance or upgrade aspect of the services)?

4.4   Which jurisdiction's laws are being referred to?
This will inevitably be dependent on the jurisdictional scope of the services, and on the deal itself. And this will usually determine the relevant jurisdictions. It will of course be necessary to consider whether the relevant jurisdictions are both those in respect of which the services are provided and the jurisdictions from which the services are provided, so that – at least from a customer perspective – it can be satisfied that both ends of the service provider's delivery would be compliant.

As more countries impose laws relevant to the manner of providing services – especially of a technology nature – it is increasingly important to carry out an assessment that the proposed service delivery model is viable in light of legal and regulatory restrictions, and to do this at a relatively early stage so as to make sure that the negotiation effort is not misdirected and misplaced.

4.5   What happens if there is a change to laws?
If the parties have agreed the supplier laws/customer laws split articulated above, it will usually be the case that the responsibility for dealing with the changes will be as follows:
- the service provider makes such changes as are necessary to achieve compliance with the supplier laws; and
- once notified by the customer, the service provider makes such changes as are necessary to adhere to the changed customer laws, and this would usually be managed through the change control process.

If changes resulting from a change to the customer laws are to go through the change control process, it will be important from a customer's point of view that this does not hold up the compliance process or become a difficult or unbalanced negotiation. As such, the parties will also likely need to consider a mandatory change procedure, or a specific regulatory/legal change procedure.

Table 1. Changes to laws

Nature of change	For whose account
Change affecting the service provider's existence as a supplier-side entity, eg, tax changes, increased insurance requirements, costs of employment.	The service provider.
Changes affecting manner of delivering the basic scope of the services.	The service provider, unless the manner has been specifically mandated by and is unique to the customer.
Changes affecting the basic scope of the services.	The service provider, but potentially some sharing by the customer possibly by reference to a cap and/or by reference to sharing the cost across a pool of affected customers.
Changes generated by the customer laws.	The customer, but apportioned across the affected supplier customer base.
Incremental requirements of the customer over and above basic compliance.	The customer.

The costs can often be shared as well, either between the parties or a broader class of the service provider's customers, depending on the nature of the change. There will be some changes which the customer will expect, and suppliers will usually accept these as being for the service provider's account. In this regard, a possible formulation is outlined in Table 1.

While compliance with laws accordingly seems a relatively straightforward principle, it is, in practice, one of most heavily nuanced provisions, resulting in some of the most detailed negotiations in IT and sourcing contracts. Paying particular attention to the nature of the services and the solution will inevitably help break any deadlock and allow the parties to come to fair positions based on skillset, experience and detailed requirements. Either way, and as noted at the start of the chapter, it is very important to remember that a compliance with laws provision will not be a 'silver bullet' from a customer perspective to achieving a broader compliance objective, and there is an increasing demand on assessing solutions and how they fit within the customer organisation to ensure that more definitive compliance assessments take place with confidence.

4. Service level agreements

1. **Introduction**

   Technology related contracts and various forms of outsourcing, cloud or managed services agreements will typically contain many provisions and warranties which relate to the quality or standard of performance that will be required for the ongoing provision of services (as opposed to the standard for acceptance of a one-off or specified work product or deliverable, where the standard to be achieved can be documented in a set of requirements or specifications and then made subject to an acceptance or approvals regime). For example, there may be a commitment to provide services 'with reasonable skill and care', and/or 'in accordance with good industry standards'. However, such commitments can be difficult to assess or quantify with any real certainty, and so create doubt as to practical enforceability.

   Accordingly, many contracts for ongoing service delivery of one kind or another will seek to go down to a lower level of detail and actually quantify/specify the actual levels of performance to be achieved, and which are commonly then referred to as 'service levels' (although the exact terminology may vary; for example, they may be referred to as key performance indicators (KPIs)).

   The task of defining and agreeing such service levels can be a major undertaking, in and of itself. However, there are then a host of related contract and operational issues to be negotiated and agreed.

2. **Service level models**

   One of the first areas for consideration – before we then get into the respective viewpoints of customer and supplier – is what service level model will be used (albeit that this will only really matter in the event that the service level regime has some degree of teeth to it in the form of sanctions for non-performance, as discussed in more detail later in this chapter). There are numerous options in this regard.

2.1 Simple service level values

This model assumes a set service level, with an equally fixed service credit that will then accrue by way of a reduction to the supplier's charges if it is not met (eg, if Service Level A is missed to any degree, then the customer will receive a pre-agreed service credit in the amount of £x). This model has the benefit of simplicity, but is relatively blunt in the sense that it does not then track any worsening performance by the supplier (eg, the service provider pays the same amount, whether it misses the service level by a whisker, or by a country mile), and also inflexible in the sense that any amendment to the value of the service credit (eg, if the deal size were to increase or volumes go up) would need to be separately negotiated and agreed.

2.2 Pool Allocation Percentage Model

Under this model, a 'pool' is created (usually expressed as a percentage of the amount placed at risk to the payment of service credits in the relevant month, and which can be more than 100% of it) which is then allocated across the various available service levels. To take a simple example, if there was a pool of 150%, 10 available service levels and they were all perceived to be of equal importance, then the pool might be split equally across them all, such that each would have an assignment of 15% of the at-risk amount to each of the service levels. If the relevant service level is missed, the assigned percentage of the overall at-risk amount is then accrued. However, on the basis that if the month's performance might then notionally come up with a figure of more than 100% – if the pool itself is greater than 100% – the supplier can never actually be asked to incur/pay more than 100% of the relevant at-risk amount. Accordingly, while having a larger pool may increase the risk that the supplier will accrue service credits up towards the top end of the at-risk amount cap, it does not increase the maximum that can be incurred. The logic of this approach – from the customer perspective at least – is that it also avoids the situation where the service provider would need to breach all of the service levels, in order for the customer to recover the full at-risk amount of service credits (as would be the case if there was only a pool of 100% of the service credit at-risk amount to then be spread across the applicable service levels).

Proponents of the Pool Allocation Percentage Model point to its flexibility, as it usually comes with a governance mechanism which allows the customer to reallocate its original divvying-up of the pool across the various service levels, so as to reflect any changes in its priorities or perceptions as to what is really important (on a 'rob Peter to pay Paul' basis, that is, any increase in an allocation of pool allocation weighting to one service level must be matched by corresponding reductions elsewhere). A point for negotiation then will be, firstly, how often such adjustments can be made (eg, annually, twice per annum or quarterly), and, secondly, whether there is a limit on how much can be shifted from one service level to another, and indeed whether there is a maximum allocation that can be made to any individual service level in any event.

If there is a key criticism of the Pool Allocation Percentage Model (at least in its vanilla, non-bespoked form), it is that it is a blunt instrument. In that it provides for the full value of the assigned pool allocation to become due if a service level is missed, regardless of whether the service level has been missed by a whisker or a country mile.

2.3   Service Credit Point Scheme

With the Service Credit Point Scheme, the parties agree a notional value of a service credit 'point', usually by dividing the at-risk amount by an agreed nominator. So, for example, if the at-risk amount to service credits were to be 10% and a monthly charge were to £10,000, the full amount at risk to service credits in that month would be £1,000; if the agreed nominator was then 200, each service credit point would be worth £5.

The parties then go through the proposed service levels and in relation to each one, assign a set of points that will accrue, depending on how far below the required service level the supplier may fall (and usually on an increasing scale). So, for example, if there was a service level which required the supplier to achieve a specific result or timescale 95% of the time, the parties might agree that the supplier would accrue one service credit point for each percentage below the required service level between 95% and 90%, two service credit points for each percentage between 90% and 85%, and then perhaps five service credit points for each lower percentage thereafter. As with the Pool Allocation Percentage Model, however, no matter how many service credit points become notionally due in a relevant measurement period, the supplier can never be asked to pay more than the agreed at-risk amount.

The benefit of such a regime is that, as with the Pool Allocation Percentage Model, the amounts at risk and their split across the service levels automatically flexes with the value of the deal. As opposed to the Pool Allocation Percentage Option, it also is perhaps a better reflection of commercial fairness in the sense that the supplier might legitimately expect not to be incurring too much by way of service credits if it is only marginally below the required service level. On the downside, however, the scheme requires a lot more detailed modelling and assessment on a service level by service level basis, and any adjustments to the rates of accrual of service credit points post contract signature will likely be subject to agreement by way of the change control process.

3. The customer perspective

3.1 The starting service levels

The customer will want to know that, as from the day that its services commence, it will be able to rely upon the service level regime as being the standard of performance it will receive. As such, the customer will usually be against any suggestion of service levels only applying upon some later point in time (either because of a need to do 'baselining', if the supplier is taking on some existing functions in an outsource style arrangement, or otherwise as a result of some form of 'observance' period when the supplier might say that it would be monitoring and reporting upon service performance, but would not have any fixed responsibility to achieve any particular service level).

Much will depend here on the nature of the services. Where the customer is engaging a supplier to provide a new service from its own networks or infrastructure (as would be the case with a software as a service (SaaS) solution, for example), then there would be no obvious reason why the service levels should not apply from the outset. However, the position may be different if the supplier is taking on systems or processes which the customer has itself been using, and if the customer does not have adequate data as to its historic performance (see supplier viewpoint on this point, below).

3.2 Do service credits apply, and, if so, with what cap?

Although there is obviously some benefit in having service levels reported in and of themselves (eg, so as to form the basis for relationship discussions and to enable the customer to form a clearer view as to the services it is receiving), the customer will ideally want the service level regime also to provide a concrete incentive to maintain the services at the required performance levels. This brings us on to the question of service credits (as already touched upon in the context of the different potential service level regimes, as discussed above).

Put simply, from a customer perspective, service credits are a reduction to the supplier's charges to reflect a failure to provide the services to the required performance standards; if a price has been set at £100 in anticipation of receiving a 100% level of service and in fact only a 95% is being achieved, then logically (it will be argued), the fee should then be adjusted downwards to £95. The customer will therefore argue that there has to be a financial consequence of the supplier not meeting a service level, both to reflect the logic of the position as outlined above and to ensure that the supplier genuinely will work to ensure that the service level is met (as it will suffer a margin impact if it does not).

The customer would likewise prefer that there then be no limit or cap on the amount of the service credits that can become payable. While there are some exceptional projects where this position may be agreed, the market norm however is for there to be some kind of cap (often then described in the contract as the at-risk amount or something similar), expressed as a percentage of the fees. Higher level/aspirational caps will be in the 17.5% range (and rare examples may even be above that).

3.3 What is included in the calculation of the at-risk amount?
The customer will want the simplicity of being able to simply refer to a percentage of the relevant monthly charges (whether they be expressed on a fixed or variable basis) *vis-à-vis* the period to which the service credits relate, that is, as a percentage of the total invoice value.

3.4 Are service credits a 'sole and exclusive' remedy?
The customer will want to resist any suggestion that service credits are its sole remedy in the event of a breach of the service levels. A service level breach may simply be symptomatic of a deeper problem or malaise, and agreeing to limit sanctions or recourse to just a payment of service credits would in effect be undermining the protection/comfort otherwise provided by the (usually much larger) damages/limitation of liability cap. The customer will therefore argue that service credits are simply a means of adjusting the relevant charges to reflect the (lower than expected) quality of service actually provided, and should be viewed entirely separately from any concept of compensation for wider loss or damage caused.

3.5 Termination triggers
If a customer has to rely upon a termination provision which allows for termination in the event of a material breach (or similar formulation), it will have to engage in a form of Russian roulette; if ultimately a court were to determine that the service provider was

not in fact in breach – or even that it was in breach, but just not so materially as to justify contract termination – then the customer will instead be viewed as the party who wrongfully terminated the contract, and will have to pay damages to the service provider.

Accordingly, there is considerable attraction for the customer to use the service level regime to remove this risk and ambiguity as to when a termination right has or has not arisen. This can be done by specifying certain levels or types of service level defaults which will automatically then be deemed to be a sufficiently material default as to justify contract termination (and on the basis that such termination triggers can be established as a simple matter of mathematical fact, and without the need for further argument as to the 'materiality' of the service provider's defaults).

Common examples of such service level related termination triggers include:

- breaching the same service level more than [X] times in any [Y] consecutive monthly period, or more than [Z] months in succession;
- breaching more than [A] service levels, in the aggregate, across any [B] number of months;
- breaching a service level (or potentially a reduced number of particularly important service levels) to a particularly serious degree, for example, if a service level was set at 90% achievement such that service credits began to accrue once performance dropped below 90%, the termination trigger might kick in if performance dropped below 80%; and
- hitting the at-risk amount regarding the incurring of service credits in a particular month more than a set number of times in a given period, or incurring more than a certain percentage of what would potentially have been payable by way of service credits over such a period (eg, incurring 70% or more of the potentially accruable service credits over a six month period).

3.6 Continuous improvement

Service levels, which may seem to be appropriate and challenging as at contract signature, may rapidly fall behind what is appropriate or achievable, based upon improvements in technology and processes. Equally, it may be that service levels are set more by reference to a customer's historic performance levels, and the service provider is then able to improve significantly upon them in the medium to longer term.

The customer will then ideally want the service levels to adapt and grow to reflect these factors. As more of a blunt instrument, the customer might seek to build into the contract some pre-set improvements to the service levels which will kick in after an agreed period of time (eg, so as to allow for the service provider to implement a degree of transformation/improvement to the service delivery). Alternatively, we have seen and negotiated provisions which tie improvements to the level of service actually achieved (eg, such that if the service provider is able to achieve a better level of service over time, the service level then automatically improves to reflect this). So, for example, if a service level was set at 90% but the actual service delivery achieved over a set period (usually annually) was actually 94%, the service level for the following year would then be uplifted by a percentage of the delta between the original service level and the level of service actually achieved; thus if the agreed uplift was 25%, in the example above the service level for the following year would be increased to 91%.

3.7 Exclusions and relief

Clearly, the customer will want to have as much certainty as possible in terms of the applicability of the service levels, and so will want to have as few exceptions or limitations to the operation of the service level regime as is possible. The customer will point to the operation of the relief events provisions in the contract, where they have been included (see Chapter 7 in this regard), and will argue that this should be the route for the service provider to follow, if it believes that it has been precluded from complying with the service levels by reason of something that the customer has not done (or potentially by reason of an event of *force majeure*).

3.8 Linked obligations

Just getting a payment of a service credit is not the whole ball game for the customer, and indeed may be of scant consolation for the impact upon the customer's business.

Customers will therefore often press for express obligations upon the service provider to investigate and rectify the underlying causes of service level failures, and to produce detailed root cause analyses to establish that this has been done. This will often also be linked to obligations upon the service provider to escalate the service level failures to more senior executives within the service provider's company (potentially even up to board level), or perhaps to ensure that such figures have visibility of the issues arising with the customer's contract by requiring that – at least in certain more serious circumstances – they have to physically attend a 'remediation' meeting, or personally sign a cheque for the relevant service credit amounts rather than simply have such sums deducted from the next available invoice.

4. The service provider perspective

4.1 The starting service levels

Where the service provider is providing a pre-existing solution (eg, in the form of a SaaS-based service), its service level offering will usually be in the form of a commodity style arrangement, with service levels set in the same form across multiple different clients. The service provider will then be loath to make any changes either to the service levels or their descriptions or modes of measurement, on the basis that this would then detract from the efficiencies of scale and ease of administration which are inherent to such service offerings. The service provider will then argue that the pricing for the services is inherently linked to the service levels which are on offer, such that the customer cannot expect to have improved or different service levels in return for the price which it is paying.

Different arguments arise when the service provider is taking over a service or function which was previously being undertaken by the customer, as with most forms of technology or business process outsourcing deal. The service provider will first want to know whether the customer has sufficient historic data to evidence what level of performance was being achieved in the past (and will typically want at least 12 months of such data, in order to assess the impact of any seasonal variations or periodic events). If it does not, then the service provider will argue that it will need to undertake such measurements itself during a post-contract signature baselining period, and that service levels (and service credits) will not be able to become effective until after such baselining has been completed. The duration of such baselining will also be the subject of much negotiation; the service provider may again begin by arguing for a 12-month period, for the exact same reasons that it will want the historic data for.

Even if the customer has historic data, it is not necessarily the end of the story insofar as the service provider is concerned. It is tempting for a customer to argue that if it can show that, over a 12-month period, it has achieved an average performance of (for example) resolving Priority 2 defects within eight hours for 85% of the time, then that should be set as the service level going forward. However, if we remember that service levels are more often than not then measured on a monthly basis, a savvy service provider will realise (and point out) that if the service level was set out in this way and the service provider then performed exactly as the customer had done historically, then on a purely statistical basis, it is quite possible (and even likely) that the service provider will be in breach of the service levels roughly six months out of the 12 in the course of the year, and so will inevitably incur service credits (and quite possibly be exposed to potential termination triggers as well). The service provider will therefore want to apply a more nuanced or sophisticated assessment of what 'historic performance' should be taken to be. To take one recent example we have seen, the service provider argued that it should only be obliged to meet the fourth highest monthly performance level as achieved by the customer itself over a six-month period.

4.2 Do service credits apply, and, if so, with what cap?

In many cases (and in particular for lower value or more commodity style technology services), the service provider will resist the idea of service credits applying in the event of any service level failures, that is, such that the service levels are simply a reporting/governance mechanism, with no additional express contractual significance. Often, they will then be drafted on the basis that the service provider will use reasonable endeavours to achieve the service levels, or will be described as 'targets'. The service provider argument will often be that its charging structure and lower fees are predicated upon the degree of risk it is willing to take on, which does not then include the financial risk of having to potentially pay out service credits.

On larger or more complex deals where this logic will not apply (or where the customer is otherwise able to argue that its imperative of ensuring ongoing quality of service means that it needs to have the comfort/incentive of knowing that the service provider has some financial 'skin in the game'), the service provider will focus its attention upon restricting the amount at risk to as small a percentage of the relevant charges as possible; percentages as low as 2.5% of monthly charges have been seen, but a more common range for supplier-led regimes is between 5% to 10%.

4.3 What is included in the calculation of the at-risk amount?

Nearly as important as the size of the cap on the at-risk amount is what it is assessed against, and perhaps surprisingly this is not always focused upon quite as much as it ought to be. In order to better protect themselves, service providers might consider expressly excluding the following from the service credit calculations:

- taxes;
- expenses;
- pass through costs (eg, regarding reseller arrangements for third-party licences, etc); and
- amortised costs (such as transition costs incurred up front but only charged over the longer term of the deal, and which accordingly would not directly relate to the services provided during the period when the relevant service credits are incurred).

4.4   Are service credits a 'sole and exclusive' remedy?

One of the most obvious downsides for a service provider as a result of a service credit regime is that they are incurred regardless of whether the customer has actually suffered any form of financial detriment as a result of the service level default or not. Depending on the way in which the service level regime has been set up, the service provider could even end up incurring the full at-risk amount even though in actual fact it has only dipped below the required level of performance across a range of different metrics by little more than a whisker. The service provider argument may accordingly be that as a *quid pro quo* for it accepting that risk, any service credits it pays should be the sole liability it incurs for service level failures (leaving the customer free, however, to argue that other provisions of the contract may have been breached, so as to then justify other compensation claims or termination rights, to the extent that it is able to). The service provider will say in this regard that it would be more appropriate to treat service credits as a form of liquidated damages, such that the parties are in effect agreeing that the service credits payable are an appropriate remedy for the service level defaults to which they relate.

4.5   Termination triggers

The service provider will want to avoid express termination triggers for service level breaches if at all possible, and will argue that the customer should instead rely upon the more generic 'material breach' related termination rights (on the basis that it would be reasonable to require the customer to make out a case that any particular service level default is in fact material in the context of the overall agreement, at the time that the relevant issues arise).

The service provider may also point out that many of the service level termination triggers can turn out to be particularly harsh in practice. To take one example, while it may superficially appear reasonable to argue for a right to terminate a contract if a service level is breached three or more times in a rolling six-month period (on the basis of characterising this as 'persistent failure'), would this still be the case if, firstly, only one service level was being breached out of a total of (say) 20 or more, and, secondly, the 'miss' in question was only a fraction in each case, such that the customer's business would barely have noticed the difference in any event. The larger the project/contract in question, the harder the service provider will likely fight against such a construct.

4.6 Continuous improvement

The service provider viewpoint in terms of improvement of service levels will often be that while improvement in terms of performance is possible in theory, the reality may be more complex. If improvements are possible at all, they may be dependent upon the customer making its own changes (whether to its systems, processes or ways of working), or may otherwise require additional investments which the customer may not wish to underwrite, and which the service provider has not otherwise accounted for in its pricing.

The service provider may also argue hard against a mechanism to increase service levels based upon past performance. Such an approach would be counter-intuitive, the service provider may say, in that it effectively penalises the service provider for over achieving against the service levels, by reason of the fact that it increases the risk of the service provider incurring service credits in the periods that follow any upwards adjustment to the service levels. On that basis, the service provider will argue, it will be positively disincentivised to look to find ways to improve the services, to the ultimate detriment of the customer's business.

4.7 Exclusions and relief

There are a range of circumstances which the service provider may point to as being a basis for granting relief against the potential application of service levels and/or service credits.

As mentioned above, the most common basis for relief is if the customer has no historical data to support its proposed service levels, leading to the need for some form of baselining period. Even if such data is available, however, the service provider may still argue that there should be a period of time where – even if the service levels are being monitored and reported against – no service credits should apply (often referred to as a 'honeymoon' period). The service provider perspective in this regard is that in the early days of engagement with the customer (and particularly if there is a substantive transition process being gone through), its primary focus will be on service continuity and bedding things down, and as such the parties should reasonably anticipate a degree of disruption and fluctuation in service performance as things settle in.

Regardless of whether or not the parties agree on such a honeymoon arrangement, there will be other exceptions that the service provider may press for, including:

- *Low numbers exceptions.* If a service level is expressed on a percentage basis (eg, requiring 80% compliance, etc) but there are a low number of relevant instances/calculation points during the measurement period in question (eg, only four or five), even a single failure by the service provider would then give rise to a service level breach. Service providers will therefore want to insert wording to adjust any such calculation mechanisms so as to ensure that (as a minimum) single defaults will not automatically give rise to service level breaches.

- *Customer dependencies.* If there are things that the service provider will need the customer to do in order to enable it to meet the service levels, the service provider will want them to be set out in the contract and to have a right of relief if the customer does not then perform as expected. Obvious examples may include the provision/availability of customer IT systems upon which the relevant services may be dependent or with which they may need to interact, but the extent of such obligations will necessarily vary from project to project.

- *Chess clock.* In some cases, the service provider's performance may be measured on an end-to-end basis but may actually include the inputs of third parties for whom the service provider does not have contractual responsibility. For example, there may be a service level which requires a resolution for an incident to be provided with a set period (say 48 hours), but the service provider may within that period need to, firstly, obtain from the customer additional information regarding the incident in question, and/or, secondly, liaise with a third-party licenser (if, for example, the incident in question goes to the source code of their licensed product). In those cases, the service provider will want to put the time calculation on hold while it is, justifiably, awaiting a response from such other parties (eg, as per the tapping of a chess clock to stop the clock ticking while the player awaits his opponent to make his move).

4.8 Linked obligations

The service provider will argue that the service credit remedy is risk enough for its performance against the service levels, such that an abundance of other linked obligations is unnecessary. It will argue that some service level defaults are not, by their nature, remediable as such and so it would be unreasonable to require it to try to do so, and/or that some service level breaches are not sufficiently material or persistent so as to justify the additional time and effort that would be entailed in having to carry out and document a full root cause analysis.

5. Potential solutions

5.1 The starting service levels

As noted above, much will depend on what data the customer has about its historic service level performance. Accepting the point that the service provider may make about simply applying the 'average' service level achieved over the relevant period in the past, we have seen mechanisms which eliminate outlier results (positive and minus) and then require the service provider to meet the median (or just under median) performance, but on the basis that it will then commit to improve the service level to the average level achieved over a longer period of time.

5.2 Do service credits apply, and, if so, with what cap?

If the engagement is of the size/complexity that merits or justifies having a service credit regime, potential compromise positions that can then be considered include:

- Whether the service provider could have a chance to 'earn back' service credits incurred in a given month, if it then meets (or possibly exceeds) the affected service level consistently over a period of time (eg, if it incurs a service credit in January for Service Level A, it can then earn back such service credit if it then meets Service Level A in each of the following six months).
- Whether there is an additional opportunity for the service provider to receive an actual cash 'upside' for overperformance,

by way of what would amount to a service bonus. While many customers we come across initially resist this concept (not least because of the budgetary challenges it may present), there are certainly at least some examples where having such a structure would make sound commercial sense. For example, if the service level related to an aspect of the customer's operations where overperformance against the required service level would likely give rise to a financial benefit for the customer, then sharing some of that benefit with the service provider by way of a service level bonus may be a win-win, and may make it easier for the service provider to then accept more of the potential service credit related downside regarding poor performance.

The resolution of those issues will also help with the discussion as to the size of the at-risk amount. In our experience, for major engagements a range of 12.5% to 15% is common (at least for managed service/outsourcing engagements; the numbers tend to be lower for 'X as a service' engagements). Larger percentages are rare, but not unknown (especially in highly competitive procurement processes).

5.3 What is included in the calculation of the at-risk amount?

As the service credits are intended to be a sharp stick to poke in the ribs of the service provider *vis-à-vis* its own performance, it would seem reasonable to exclude taxes and expenses from the calculation. Equally, if one-off costs have been amortised over a contract (and which therefore don't really relate to the performance of the services in the month in question), it would seem reasonable to exclude them from the service credit calculation. However, more generic 'project management' charges seem to be more closely linked to the services and therefore more reasonable to include.

5.4 Are service credits a 'sole and exclusive' remedy?

As a matter of reality, customers are not usually too quick to rush to claim compensation from their service providers, over and above whatever amounts of service credits have accrued, in the event of there being service level issues, at least unless things have got seriously bad. The parties could therefore consider finding some language to seek to reflect this practical reality in contractual terms, for example, by agreeing that the customer can claim damages in addition, but only when certain thresholds are met. Examples we have seen include:

- where the at-risk amount (or a set proportion/percentage of it) has accrued in a given measurement period;
- if the relevant service level has not just been missed, but has been missed by a particular (and more serious) degree; and
- where the loss attributable to the default itself exceeds an agreed threshold value.

In any event, we ordinarily see agreement to the proposition that the amounts of service credits paid for a particular service level breach should be offset against claims of damages for the same underlying causes.

5.5 Termination triggers

Where the service level agreement is to have linked termination rights, the key compromise is to ensure that the level set is genuinely comparable to what could be said to be a 'material' breach. To take an example, a termination trigger linked to the breach of the same service level three times in a row may seem reasonable. However, would it be truly fair to see a contract terminated for breach if that was then the only service level being breached, and in fact it was only being missed by a hair's breadth on each occasion?

In practice, therefore, where there are to be termination triggers linked to non-performance against individual service levels, it would be reasonable for each such service level default to have been to more than a minor degree, in order to count towards the termination trigger.

5.6 Continuous improvement

The service provider argument that automatic increases in the service levels creates a disincentive to seeking overperformance is a fair one (albeit a service provider will also aim to overachieve in any event, so as to provide a degree of buffer against isolated problems). However, this could be overcome by looking to, firstly, elongate the period over which the performance is measured, and/or, secondly, to reduce the amount of the increase in the service level which then results (eg, increasing by 25% of the delta between the historic service level and the newly established level of actual performance, rather than 50%). The pain the service provider may feel may also be offset by potentially providing for a level of bonus payment at the end of the year if it has managed to demonstrate such a level of over performance (see comments above as to potential win-win benefits for both the customer and service provider). The customer can of course in any event seek to build in a continuous improvement programme whereby the service provider is obliged to bring forward proposals for service level performance, albeit potentially then on the basis that some improvements may need funding via the Change Control Procedure.

For projects which are susceptible to benchmarking (see Chapter 10), it is worth noting that if the service provider does not improve the service levels in line with what is generally achievable in the market, this may become a factor in the assessment of the benchmarked charges.

5.7   Exclusions and relief

Where the customer has dependencies, it may be willing to grant relief but will likely wish to argue for the same kind of discipline as applies to other claimed customer defaults, ie so as to require it to be notified on a timely basis of what it is said to have not been doing, or not to have been doing right.

Where exceptions for the inputs of third parties are argued for, it is superficially easy to accept that they should apply. However, a word of caution (and a reasonable caveat to them); if the service levels are being set on the basis of historic experience/performance, and such records already take into account the factors of customer response times and/or inputs from third parties, then there would be a risk that providing the service provider with a further degree of relief (whether via the chess clock measure or otherwise) would in effect provide it with double relief. The customer may in such circumstances reasonably query why it would be the case that its personnel or those of third-party suppliers would start to be less timely with their inputs and responses, simply because of the fact that they are dealing with the supplier.

5.8   Linked obligations

It is fair to say that not all service level defaults can be retrospectively addressed, and equally more minor service levels do not need full root-cause analysis (and the customer would probably not read them, even if they were produced). Having such obligations respectively limited to services which are actually capable of being re-performed and to service defaults which are more serious or repetitive in nature therefore feels reasonable.

Escalations to senior executives also need to be addressed with some degree of perspective. The reality is that many supplier contract managers will have their careers damaged by having apparent poor performance flagged up to their superiors by reason of them being pulled into calls or meetings to help explain the problems (if that is what the contract provides), and imposing this obligation upon them at anything less than a serious level of non-performance is likely to engender unhelpful and overly defensive behaviours on their part, to the likely detriment of the project as a whole.

5. Use of agile methodologies

1. Introduction

1.1 Agile contracting

Agile software development is fundamentally different from traditional processes, and as such, the contract terms which accompany agile development are also subtly different in many ways.

Agile development methodologies of one form or another have been around for many years. However, in recent years we have seen an uptick in the use of agile methods in both the public and private sector (largely it would appear because of its promise to enable faster project delivery, which fits well with the speed driven imperatives of digital transformation projects, in particular). Yet, knowledge and awareness of agile-typical styles and consequential contract terms has lagged behind. This comparative lack of knowledge/sophistication tends to be because most large-scale technology contracts (outsourcing or otherwise) have been run alongside traditional or waterfall methods of solution development. Those traditional methods will, in one form or another, have a set of customer requirements, which are passed over the fence to a group of suppliers to tender upon, and then the requirements and solution are written into a contract as a *fait accompli*. Indeed, in broad terms, the approach of an outsourcing customer has been one to ask the service provider, with metaphoric folded arms, to prove what it can do, to show the customer what it has paid for. That disconnect between the two parties has been at the heart of the rise of agile methods.

Agile was originally born out of software developers' frustration with the huge number of failed IT projects that they attributed to the flawed approach of traditional waterfall methodologies. The result of which included millions of pounds worth of lost fees; delays of up to several years; and uninspired and demotivated project teams. While its roots are in software development, the biggest proponents of agile would argue that it should be used in everything from building infrastructure to expanding human resources. This is predicated on the assumption that agile accelerates human effort and therefore it doesn't matter what the effort is (ie, it has universal application).

Agile development and waterfall development methodologies are forms of development process for large-scale, complex projects. Any methodology (eg, such as PRINCE2, SSADM, Kanban, DSDM, RAD and so forth) is a way of breaking up a huge problem into manageable sections. To understand agile techniques, it is useful to distinguish them from the waterfall approach.

1.2 The waterfall approach

When using a traditional or waterfall approach, the project is divided into stages. The activity passes from one stage to another, often represented visually as a series of steps (mirroring the shape of a waterfall) as can be seen in Figure 1.

The criticism of this approach is that you need a reasonably certain set of requirements to use it properly. But real life is more complicated than that and so the rigidity of the waterfall approach can often fail to deliver a successful project where requirements are more nebulous. Indeed, if the customer actually needs to employ the skills of the technology supplier to understand the art of the possible, then a far more collaborative approach is required. In other words, an agile approach.

Figure 1. Stages in the waterfall approach

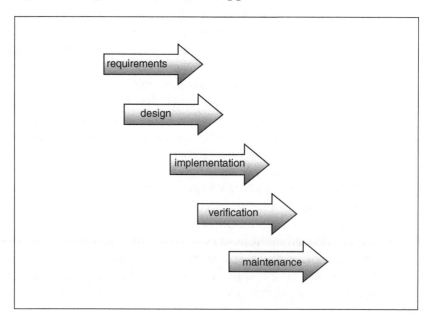

1.3 Agile development

Perhaps the most widely accepted definition of the agile approach comes from the Agile Manifesto, published in 2001. This manifesto came about when 17 software developers met at a resort in Snowbird, Utah in 2001 in order to discuss alternative development methods. It resulted in their signing of the manifesto and the creation of the following 12 Principles:[1]

Our highest priority is to satisfy the customer through early and continuous delivery of valuable software.

Welcome changing requirements, even late in development. Agile processes harness change for the customer's competitive advantage.

Deliver working software frequently, from a couple of weeks to a couple of months, with a preference to the shorter timescale.

Business people and developers must work together daily throughout the project.

Build projects around motivated individuals. Give them the environment and support they need, and trust them to get the job done.

The most efficient and effective method of conveying information to and within a development team is face-to-face conversation.

Working software is the primary measure of progress.

Agile processes promote sustainable development. The sponsors, developers, and users should be able to maintain a constant pace indefinitely.

Continuous attention to technical excellence and good design enhances agility.

Simplicity – the art of maximizing the amount of work not done – is essential.

The best architectures, requirements, and designs emerge from self-organizing teams.

At regular intervals, the team reflects on how to become more effective, then tunes and adjusts its behavior accordingly.

---

1 © Agile Alliance, www.agilealliance.org/agile101/12-principles-behind-the-agile-mani festo/. For full details of the manifesto and its signatories, see www.agilemanifesto.org.

The following ideals can be taken from the Agile Manifesto: an embracing of change, continuous delivery, speed of service, trust between all relevant stakeholders, reflection and iteration. These foundations are difficult to argue with. However, a different perspective (collaboration, joint work, speed and trust) can be sensed here, which will have an impact on the traditional rights and obligations of a sourcing agreement.

The values they agreed on through the manifesto are as follows:

- tools and processes are important, but it is more important to have competent people working together effectively;
- good documentation is useful in helping people to understand how the software is built and how to use it, but the main point of development is to create software not documentation;
- a contract is important but there is no substitute for working closely with customers to discover what they need; and
- a project plan is important but it must not be too rigid; it should be able to accommodate changes in technology or the environment, stakeholders' priorities and people's understanding of the problem and its solution.

For our purposes, it is best to think of agile as a catch-all term covering all of the different means of addressing the aims of the Agile Manifesto. Lift the lid and there are many different flavours of agile development contained within involving alien terms such as scrum, sprint and backlog. At its heart the agile approach is the approach of collaboration: customer and service provider working together to deliver success. That means shared responsibility (as opposed to blame) and a far greater degree of trust and collaboration. So, how does that work with a traditional contract structure where rights and responsibilities are set out in a way that can be measured simply? How can the customer blame the service provider for poor performance if it has been heavily involved in the development process? Also, how can the service provider know when it has completed its work if there is no defined point of acceptance?

1.4   How agile works in practice

Terminology varies but the stages are relatively consistent across the different flavours of agile methodology.

Typically, some sort of 'project vision' will be agreed by both the customer and the service provider. Then an 'agile team' will be established, led by a 'product owner' who is the customer's main representative for all decisions concerning the project. The team will meet in short, focused sessions which are often referred to as 'scrums'.

In parallel, a service provider will appoint a leader. In certain flavours of agile development, this is called the 'scrum master'. This leader will run the development team to develop the required solution. The co-creator of this team (or 'scrum') approach (Jeff Sutherland) has argued that, to get started, all you need is a broad vision of what it is you want to achieve and a backlog of everything that needs to be built or achieved at a high level in order to make that vision a reality. So instead of siloed teams being responsible for each phase of a project (ie, discovery, design, build and testing) everyone who is needed to achieve that vision will be on the agile team.

Under the 'scrum framework', the scrum team are afforded the autonomy to decide what they do, how and when. They organise themselves which can be a daunting prospect for senior management. There are guardrails that are imposed around this:

- a scrum master is appointed to coach the rest of the team through the scrum framework and eliminate anything that is slowing them down; and
- a product owner has the vision of what the team is going to do, make or accomplish.

They both take into account the risks and rewards, what is possible, what can be done and what they are passionate about. The product owner will be someone within the customer's organisation (or someone who is appointed to act on their behalf). As may be anticipated, it is the joint nature of these activities that can present difficulties from a contractual perspective.

The development team itself is responsible for the design, creation, development, configuration and integration of the developed software and the implementation of what are known as 'product backlog items'.

The development work by the team will be undertaken in stages; often termed 'sprints' and the outcome of each sprint is usually referred to as an 'increment'. The sprints will work on identified user stories and are often of limited duration, for example, two weeks, and the throughput of activity is referred to as 'velocity'. The sprint work and development project will be set against an overall 'release plan' agreed by both customer and service provider which sets out the overall plan for the development project, identifying the minimum viable product (MVP) (or similarly termed 'target outcome').

What is apparent from the above, if we look underneath the unfamiliar terminology, is that the same steps as the traditional waterfall model are being undertaken, but on an iterative and far quicker basis. How then is this sort of project contracted for? The key challenges for the conclusion of a sensible agile contract are as follows:

- agile is intended to be inherently flexible;
- it is seen by IT teams as a journey (the contract needs to allow for flexibility and innovation); and
- the contract needs to provide protection against scope creep, delay and budget pressure.

The customer and service provider will have differing perspectives as to how to balance risk and reward in a suitable contract.

2.   The customer perspective

Customers will want to ensure that (what they perceive to be) a new contracting style can still cover off their concerns. Such concerns will include the following.

- *Clarity.* How will key stakeholders agree to a business case where there is a lack of clarity about the end game and individual roles? Customers are used to clear statements of responsibility, milestones and acceptance procedures. With agile, there is less clear assignment of responsibility for different phases or the assurance that the parties will achieve exactly what they hope they will achieve.
- *Challenges to traditional mindset.* The transition from waterfall to agile involves a completely different mindset. The traditional planning approach can be hard to forego where the individuals concerned have only ever used waterfall.
- *Skills gap.* Not many customer organisations will have agile development experience and that means that there is a language barrier and potential suspicion that the customer will not achieve a value for money deal.
- *Collaboration challenge.* The two contracting parties will have different commercial interests and so the idea that collaboration is central to agile development is at odds with that fact. As such, joint working requires a change of approach and change of attitude to risk.
- *Testing overhead.* Iterative testing is an essential feature of agile development but this means extra engagement and allocation of resource by the customer.

3. The service provider perspective

The service provider will similarly have a number of key concerns for an agile project.

- *Cashflow.* The service provider will be establishing an agile development team for the customer and so will instantly have a workforce overhead which must be paid for. As such, the payment mechanism will need to reflect the set-up elements for the service provider, instead of waiting until some form of formal acceptance and/or payment by milestone achievement.
- *Dependencies and assumptions.* The reliance upon collaboration with the customer's team means that successful delivery is not solely within the hands of the service provider. As such, carefully crafted assumptions and dependencies will be essential if the service provider is to protect its profit stream and avoid becoming in breach of its contractual obligations, and with associated relief wording to be clear.

4. Potential solutions

Before adopting an agile approach, consideration should be given to whether an agile approach is suitable for the project at hand.

4.1 The requirements

A key factor is the requirement specification. Is this a project where requirements can be specified up front to a degree of accuracy, allowing the supply community to bid against a requirement and resulting in a contract that will pay for good work done? Will it offer the customer rights and remedies in the event of lateness, poor performance, undelivered functionality and so forth? If so, agile may not be appropriate. By contrast, where there is a vision as to where the customer would like to get to and an urgency to get there, but little else in terms of finer detail, then it may be right for the customer community to work together with experts in the supply community to solve the problem at hand, and this will be where the use of agile can come to the fore.

4.2 What about stakeholder attitudes?

The project and the requirement status might suit an agile approach, but before launching in, serious consideration must be given to an organisation's attitude to change. If the culture of an organisation, and that of the key stakeholders within that organisation, does not lend itself to innovation and instead follows strict procedures and policies, then the uncertainty associated with agile and the autonomy afforded to agile teams may present too much of a culture shock for senior leadership. As ever, stakeholder engagement and buy-in will be essential at the outset of an agile project.

4.3   Using the contract to help

While it would be wrong to advocate a waterfall contract for an agile project, there are many elements of typical drafting which can be retained. For example, the vision can be made as certain as possible. This will benefit both parties because it will contractualise the intention of the parties at the point at which the contract is struck. Also, that can be used as a reference point if disputes arise later.

At a lower level of detail, this might mean workshopping with both the customer and service provider teams to gain as much clarity as possible as to the must-have characteristics of the expected solution. If this can be done, then the broad nature of the expected minimum viable product can be sketched out (and undergoing this step will flush out misunderstandings between the parties at an early stage which is an added bonus).

A key way to help protect both customer and service provider (so as to avoid future disputes) is to consider taking a form of 'middle ground' contract style that marries some of the certainty of waterfall with the flexibility of agile. Agile purists may argue that this erodes the fluidity of agile, but defining an expected MVP can assist learning and lead to the identification of new user stories to add to the backlog. Similarly, and perhaps more importantly, having a contractually defined MVP can allow for the use of traditional rights and remedies, such as contractual timelines and consequences for non- or late delivery, together with a capped/fixed charge component for the MVP (often with a percentage tolerance to accommodate some minimal change).

4.4   Clear rules of the game

To make the project work, and irrespective of the particular agile methodology being followed, it is important for both parties to be clear on the rules of the game. So, both parties should decide up front, and capture in the contract, the process for project cycles, the sprint duration, the detail to be set out in the release notes accompanying the agile engine and the details of how incomplete items will be returned to the product backlog.

This essentially means that the contract will be clear as to responsibilities within teams. The teams themselves will need to be staffed by capable individuals (and so familiar concepts such as clauses requiring certain levels of expertise and identifying key personnel will be relevant). Project management itself should be a measured factor, with rights retained for the customer to request (or insist upon) changes to the service provider's team if unhappy with performance.

Having a suitable governance regime to oversee the agile team's progress is critical. Again, while purists may hate this approach it can help to reassure anxious executives that the project is on track. As part of this, senior stakeholders can be invited to watch periodic demos of the items that are defined as being done. Or this could form part of the iterative testing process. Having tangible working outputs can help to de-risk the project from their perspective, as this should be preferable to beautifully drafted documentation.

4.5 Performance management during the term

Service levels and key performance indicators still work for an agile development, even if they are adjusted to fit. A typical agile contract will assess factors including the following.

- *Velocity*. This is the average amount of work a team completes in a sprint, measured in points or hours.
- *Burndown*. Each sprint team will forecast the work and throughput for that particular sprint in the sprint planning phase. A sprint burndown tracks completion of work over time, and an 'epic' or 'release' burndown tracks progress over the project as a whole.
- *Backlog*. This is the number of days an item can remain on the backlog (taking account of complexity).

As regards service level agreements, the overall burn rate can be used to see how quickly product/user stories are being handed over as compared with the expected timeline. If performance is not as required then normal escalation routes can be used as a remedy. It is also possible to measure the number of defects/increments being returned to the backlog per sprint as a sign of poor development. The main protection from the customer perspective is that the service provider only gets paid when the sprints are accepted (signed off as done), or else gets a portion of fees withheld.

4.6 The right commercial model

For an agile project, it is very difficult to work to a fixed price because of the variability that arises through the development process. Equally, a pure time and materials agreement will feel like a blank cheque from the customer's perspective. So, the question is, where can a suitable middle ground be found?

The analysis here of the appropriate payment mechanism needs to track the agile process itself. One approach is to use an estimation and true-up model as follows:

- requirements are discussed and a budget is produced by the service provider, looking at the expected user stories, setting out any expected dependencies upon the customer and any third parties, together with all assumptions;
- the resultant estimating approach is then used for each programme increment;
- for each programme increment the service provider produces the estimated effort and price for implementing the user stories;
- the parties work together to prioritise the user stories and the contents of each iteration;
- the stories are then progressed in accordance with the agile development practices, time-boxing the activity;
- at the end of each iteration, the user story is inspected by the customer and the iteration is either accepted because the relevant criteria are met or is treated as unproven and payments (and retentions) can be ascribed to these eventualities; and
- by then comparing the estimated effort and the actual effort, in the context of the number of completed and accepted user stories, the customer and service provider can be clear on the charges due and payable.

4.7   Fault

Both parties need to know that the contract can support a contention that a party is not living up to expectations. However, the agile method means that responsibility for project delivery can become blurred and as a result it can be difficult to attribute blame to either party if the project doesn't proceed as anticipated.

The best way to mitigate this contractually is to set out the roles and responsibilities of each party. In addition, where the pricing model is (essentially) for the customer to pay for the service provider's agile team, rather than being attached to outputs *per se*, it is sensible to include performance measures which can adjust price. Further, a level of gainshare can be appropriate to ensure the service provider is incentivised to see the project through to conclusion.

4.8 The 'what if' scenarios

As with any contract, it will be key to be clear on the circumstances under which the service provider or customer can terminate, whether for breach or for convenience. Added to that, the normal 'consequences of termination' considerations apply to an agile process as much as a waterfall process if a project is terminated without running its full course.

- Who owns the work in progress (how is intellectual property (IP) treated)?
- What run-off obligations can the service provider agree to, in order to extricate itself in a way that is not expensive?
- What run-off assistance does the customer need to transfer the unfinished project back inhouse or to another provider?

As discussed above, agile development does not mean throwing away well-known contractual principles or changing the risk profile of an engagement so much that it becomes unachievable for a customer. Nonetheless it is not a blank cheque approach and with thought and consideration, a workable, agile-friendly contract can be constructed which balances the risk appetite of the customer without impairing the innovation and expertise of the service provider.

6. Warranties

1. Introduction

For the purposes of this chapter, 'warranties' refers to the specific clause within the agreement headed 'warranties'. There is often a heated debate as to the content of warranties but it is worth reflecting on the nature of a warranty and what it means, especially in the context of current approaches to drafting. As a matter of law (without reference to the specific terms of the agreement), a warranty is a contractual promise but one that does not carry the same consequences in the event of non-compliance as a 'condition' does, which would give rise to a right to terminate the agreement, if it were to be breached. A warranty would give rise to a claim in damages only (unless there was to be a repudiatory breach at common law, or if the contract specified separate termination rights). This distinction (and the indeterminate state of an innominate term) is largely irrelevant in modern technology and sourcing contracts by virtue of the specific rights to terminate set out in the agreement – whether by reference to material breach of any term or for breach of specific terms or the occurrence of specific events.

Additionally, it is not unusual to see (at least in first drafts from some customers) that a warranty clause is drafted as being given as a warranty and also as a 'representation' and an 'undertaking'. The benefit of a representation is that, if untrue, it creates the possibility of the innocent party being able to rely on remedies associated with misrepresentation and if that misrepresentation is given fraudulently, then under English law, this could generate a position of unlimited liability on the part of the person giving the representation and, potentially, the ability to rescind the contract on the part of the innocent party (which may in turn give rise to a different – and potentially more beneficial – calculation of loss). An undertaking is, in this context, another term for a contractual promise and so does not, of itself, add much.

This chapter looks at those warranties generally regarded as relevant to technology contracts. Naturally, as every deal is different this means that additional or differently focused warranties will be required.

2.   The customer perspective

A warranty is an important contractual promise; it articulates, with clarity, the key promises made by the service provider that underpin the relationship between them. Warranties deserve, therefore, to be relatively wide-ranging so as to set out, for absolute clarity, what the customer can expect. The warranties help to articulate key aspects that might otherwise be set out in more detail and act as a signpost to those provisions, for example, by providing for a warranty as to compliance in relation to the security provisions that might be set out in a schedule. Accordingly, the customer will want to focus on warranties as being a key area of contract, and one which plays a core role in underpinning the nature and aspects of the relationship.

This chapter does not discuss warranties in terms of the ability to contract and in relation to permissions and consents etc; these are of course as relevant to any contract as to a technology and sourcing contract. In the context of negotiating technology contracts, the main warranties the customer will likely require are set out in the remainder of this chapter.

2.1   Performance warranties

Here, there are likely to be a number of warranties that the customer would expect to see the service provider provide and these will be:

- performance of the services in accordance with a particular standard, eg, reasonable skill and care or good industry practice;
- adherence to the service levels; and
- ensuring that the outputs or deliverables comply with a specification.

2.2   Performance of the services in accordance with a performance standard

It is of course very important that the customer feels comfortable that the service provider is committed to performing an appropriate standard of care. In the absence of any standard set out in the agreement, English law provides that the performance standard would be that of reasonable care and skill. For many customers this standard will not be sufficient – it has (often) selected the service provider ahead of its peers and on the basis of direct or indirect statements as to the service provider's capability and expertise. In such a case and given the relative importance of the project to the customer, the customer will likely want to push for a higher standard, linked to a definition of 'good industry practice' that probably talks to a standard expected of 'highly' skilled individuals with a significant or material degree of experience and expertise in relation to the relevant services.

2.3 Warranty as to fitness for purpose

Under English law, a warranty as to fitness for purpose has the effect of promising that the output will meet the customer's specific demands. This is not unreasonable if the customer has made a specific purpose known to the service provider – and it is fair and reasonable that what it receives will be 'useful' in the context of the particular purpose for which the customer has engaged the service provider and paid for the outputs. It is therefore – perhaps having articulated the relevant purpose – and setting this out in the agreement, fair that the supplier commits to delivering a service or series of outputs that are fit for purpose.

2.4 Adherence to the service levels

Where the contract is for the ongoing provision of services (eg, for support and maintenance services, cloud based services or outsourced functions) the customer will want to be assured that there is a contractual commitment to meet, or exceed, the service levels which have been agreed as a means of describing the required standard/ quality of delivery, and so that it can, as required, found a contractual claim for breach of contract in the event that the service levels are not met. It will also want to be clear that the service levels are not the absolute standard of performance and so will draft the provisions on the basis that the service provider must meet, or exceed, the service levels. This additional wording focuses the performance so that the service levels become a minimum standard in the context of the remainder of the provisions of the agreement, including, therefore, the obligations to perform the services in accordance with good industry practice or other such standard as is agreed between the parties.

2.5 Compliance with specification

This warranty will be more relevant to a service that generates a particular output, for example, a particular solution or software deliverable. However, a customer will likely also expect this to apply to the ongoing outputs of the service, for example, as part of an application development outsourcing where there will be specifications or business requirements for each element of activity. This will be the case notwithstanding that there might be a form of managed service provided in respect of these outputs following their acceptance into the support model. The customer will want to be clear that if the outputs do not comply with the specification, its remedies are not simply the provision of support and any associated service levels, but a claim for loss resulting from the underlying failure to achieve the specification in the first place, which in turn might impact its business operations.

One key area of debate is the actual structure of the warranty that outlines how the output will comply with the specification. There will often be a statement of a time limit attached to it. From the customer perspective, this is, however, not a time limit on the extent of the service provider's responsibility (which it would be if the relevant drafting said: "the service provider warrants that, for a period of [X] days, the output will comply with its specification"). Rather, it is a period of time in which the customer has to notify the service provider of apparent issues and if so notified the service provider will fix, without charge (and without any argument as to whether the customer is suffering any loss or inconvenience as a result of the non-conformity). It is to be seen as a 'safety net' for the development activities and the testing processes, not an effective limit on the extent of the service provider's basic liability for what it has provided (and which could in fact be subject to challenge under Section 13 and/or Section 3 of the Unfair Contract Terms Act 1977).

2.6 Commitment to timescales

The customer is likely working with the service provider for a number of reasons including expertise and ability, but also the ability to deliver the required services and outputs quicker than it would otherwise be able to do itself. The deal itself might well be linked to achieving business objectives which might be transformative or pure cost saving in nature. It will be important that the service provider meets these deadlines, and is incentivised to do so via a contractual promise to meet deadlines, on the basis that if deadlines are missed the service provider understands that there might be some consequences to this.

As such, the service provider should warrant to deliver in accordance with a specified project or implementation plan and in doing so accept that, in addition to specific remedies as may be set out in the agreement (eg, delay payments), it should be responsible for other loss that the customer incurs as a result of the service provider's failure to deliver on time.

2.7 Warranties regarding intellectual property rights (IPR)

Even though the service provider might provide an indemnity for the customer's benefit in relation to third-party intellectual property (IP) infringement claims, the customer will also expect a warranty that its possession and use (and that of its permitted users) will not infringe the IPR of a third party, and preferably will not expose the customer (and those users) to claims of infringement from a third party. This latter part is important as it could give rise to a right to terminate in the event that the claim is actually made (and notwithstanding the indemnity which may suffice to cover its financial losses) so creating the avenue of the customer to exit the agreement for the service provider's breach of contract, which again will generate the ability for the customer to claim damages for losses incurred as a result of the termination (because the termination was then for breach of warranty).

2.8 Use of open source

Within technology projects, there remains a healthy fear of the use of open source because of the potential 'copy left' impact and the possibility that the customer's proprietary code might be subject to disclosure and licensing on the same terms as the open source software itself. Consequently, a customer will usually demand a warranty that the outputs of the services and any software or systems that are to be interfaced to or integrated with its own software or solutions will be free of open source software, or at least saved as may have been expressly agreed.

Some service providers will seek to caveat this provision by reference to a series of disclosed licence types that might apply to the software within the solution. Customers will reject this on the basis that it is not the customer's responsibility to be assured that the service provider has the relevant licence rights to enable it to comply with the terms of the agreement, including the licence rights and the non-infringement commitments.

2.9 Security

Customers will usually expect a warranty to comply with security measures that are set out in the agreement, most likely in a schedule to the agreement and consisting of security requirements relevant to the services and solution. However, these requirements are a snapshot in time and so the customer will ask the service provider also to warrant that the security requirements will meet some other standard – most likely those required by good industry practice – as that standard changes from time to time. The service provider is best placed to know what measures need to apply to its own solution – the customer cannot necessarily see or understand what is happening within the solution to be able to predict and dictate all the necessary security requirements to be imposed to it; the supplier must therefore take some responsibility for what is happening on its side of the fence.

2.10 Data protection and privacy

The commitments relating to data protection and privacy are discussed in Chapter 9 so that chapter should be referred to for a consideration of the relevant issues. The customer will want to be specifically assured that the service provider will comply with its obligations in this regard.

2.11 Compliance with laws

The customer will often press for specific assurances that the services and/or related deliverables will comply with all applicable laws and regulations. This may be particularly so in the context of ongoing services, where the customer's own compliance may be dependent upon the service provider's services.

3. The service provider perspective

Warranties should be taken seriously and given in a considered manner, making sure that they are balanced and capable of being delivered. They are not to be used as catch-all statements as to the customer's preferred positions that are not already (but perhaps should be) better dealt with via detailed and carefully structured and negotiated contract terms. As such, they need very careful consideration and should be well drafted and focused.

3.1 Performance warranties

A service provider will not be averse to committing to performance standards – it understands, after all, that part of the commercial transaction means that it is being paid in return for the performance of 'quality' services and outputs. However, 'quality' in this context needs to be contextualised, whether by reference to the solution being provided or other parts of the overall arrangements. The service provider will also want to ensure that the standards it is expected to meet are reflected by the charges it is being paid.

3.2 Performance of the services in accordance with a performance standard

Most legal systems will provide a 'default' standard that will be applied, in the absence of anything specific in the contract. For example, English law provides for a standard of performance – that of reasonable care and skill (see Section 13 of the Sale of Goods and Services Act 1982). On the basis that English law has already determined the required standard of performance to which it would be appropriate to hold suppliers, this should be the basic proposition and from which the conversation starts. Naturally, it might be relevant to agree a slightly enhanced standard, but most service providers would argue that it would not be sensible or necessary to agree a standard that is considerably higher than this. Additionally, a suggestion that the service provider should be performing at the 'highest' possible level is difficult to agree because, firstly, the customer might not be buying the most optimal solution which will enable the service provider to meet this standard and, secondly, there may be issues with understanding what the 'highest' standard is, such that the service provider knows what it needs to do, how it needs to staff a deal and how it needs to establish a particular solution in order to meet this standard.

The arguments a service provider puts forward in this regard are not to be seen as a lack of confidence in its ability or the concentration it will apply when it comes to the delivery of the service; the position with regards to the performance standard is simply a risk issue – whether the service provider should absorb a higher than necessary risk – necessary in the context of what the law actually expects and what it is capable of delivering by virtue of what choices the customer has made with regards to the service it wants to buy.

3.3 Adherence to service levels

If the service provider has already committed to meet the service levels and agreed a regime within the service level schedule and with regards to the consequences of failing to meet the service levels (ie, the payment, eg, service credits), then it may argue that the issue of not meeting the service levels is already addressed; there simply does not need to be a separate or duplicative or different (however it might be characterised) obligation. To accept this as a separate obligation would expose the service provider, potentially, to greater liability or a greater chance of having the contract terminated, in excess of what would be reasonable in light of the deal reached on the service levels themselves. So, the service provider may argue that while it will accept a potential reduction in its charges should a service level be missed, this should not be characterised as a 'breach' event.

3.4 Compliance with specification

So long as the specification is agreed, and is appropriately detailed, committing to deliver in accordance with the specification should not, in and of itself, be too much of an issue. However, there ought to be a recognition that in some cases a specification will be so detailed that it is either not practicable or makes little difference whether absolutely all the individual requirements of the specification are met so long as the key parts of it are delivered. Moreover, it would not be reasonable for the service provider to be exposed to a damages claim or even a potential termination if immaterial elements of the services or solution are not delivered, especially when in real terms there is unlikely to be much impact on the customer if the non-material elements are not delivered (on the basis if they were important that would be material). As such, the service provider would likely think it appropriate to frame a commitment to meet the specification so that it will meet the specification, in 'all material respects'.

As to the suggestion from the customer that the warranty should not be time-boxed, this would not make sense as far as the service provider is concerned. The whole purpose of providing either a managed service or support and maintenance services is to recognise that, after time, software or IT equipment can develop defects and will need some support in addressing those issues. In the same way that a car needs regular servicing, and might need parts of it replacing from time to time, so a customer would be sensible to appreciate that its outputs might need to be supported. It simply is not in the service provider's commercial model to be able to offer a service whereby it could be responsible for an output delivered several years previously (not least because this would potentially require the service provider to maintain a separate team of personnel capable of doing this).

Additionally, and as a final point, certain outputs clearly cannot be subject to an ongoing warranty – they are by their nature fixed at a moment in time, such as reports containing data – and so these clearly need to be time bound.

3.5 Commitments to timescales

As with service levels, if there is a detailed implementation schedule with associated project plan and commitments to meet that plan, then a further or distinct warranty is simply not required. Additionally, committing to meet a timescale is not as straightforward or as simple as it sounds; the ability to meet a deadline is heavily dependent on a number of external factors such as third parties or the customer itself, for which the service provider is not responsible. Additionally, what does it mean to hit a timescale? To understand whether a deadline or a milestone has been achieved, there will need to be an appropriate acceptance process which will need to have been completed in order to assess whether the timescale has been achieved. This is unlikely to be so straightforward as to allow for a simple 'yes' or 'no' assessment as to whether the timescale and the contractual commitment is delivered.

3.6 Warranties regarding IPR

On the basis the service provider gives (or is likely to give) an indemnity – in some form or another – in respect of third-party claims of IP infringement, this indemnity will set out the extent of its responsibility with regards to IP infringement and will adequately deal with any losses that the customer might incur. As such, the service provider will argue that an IP warranty is not required, especially if it's IP indemnity language also obliges it to try to resolve or provide a 'fix' for any IPR-related issue, once a claim has been made.

3.7 Use of open source

Unless the software being provided is very specific (and likely quite small in scale), it may be difficult and/or impractical for a service provider to commit not to use open source software. This will especially be the case if the service provider is utilising existing software or systems that themselves include open source. In the current market (as compared to ten or 15 years ago), open source is so prevalent, and so much better understood from both technical and legal perspectives, that the issues feared from the use of open source and that are generating the perceived 'mischief' driving the warranty are not as great as they used to be. An open source warranty can accordingly be argued to be somewhat out-dated.

To enable the customer to leverage the existing solutions of the service provider at the price the customer wants to pay (as opposed to requiring the supplier to build a bespoke solution at huge cost to the customer), it is more appropriate to recognise there may be open source and to provide details of the relevant licences so that the customer can review for itself and, if it believes necessary, take appropriate steps at its end to make sure it does not breach those terms.

3.8 Security

The key reason behind the customer requiring warranties with regards to security is to safeguard the customer's information and data, which could of course change over the term of an agreement in light of the customer's business activities or its own clients' activities. The service provider does not know the content of this information and so cannot be in a position to understand or determine what level of security or what security measures should be put in place. Provided that the customer is responsible for agreeing, in the contract, the specific measures to be implemented, the service provider will commit to meeting these, as part of the solution and service that it provides.

The service provider will be concerned about the standard it is being expected to meet – and what this actually is – but also the cost of doing so, which might far exceed the level of costs for which the supplier has budgeted such that it is unreasonable for it to expect it to bear the costs of keeping up to date with a level of security. However, that might change to meet the demands of the customer's potentially changing business.

3.9 Data protection and security

The service provider will likely be willing to warrant compliance with such data protection and security-related obligations that are agreed as at the date of contract signature. However, in the event of changes to such requirements in future (eg, by reason of changes in the customer's IT security standards), the service provider will want to have both a reasonable period of notice to enable it to comply, and likely will want to recover any additional costs associated with such changes.

3.10 Compliance with laws

Compliance with laws can be a vexed issue for service providers. Compliance as at the first day of service commencement or delivery may be one thing, but dealing with changes in laws can be more problematic. The service provider may be willing to warrant compliance with the laws which relate to it as a service provider, but may not warrant to comply with other changes in law which it may find more difficult to predict (and price for), and particularly so in relation to changes which are more specific to the customer's business sector.

4. Potential compromises

Naturally, there are a number of potential compromises to the issues raised in relation to the warranties. One of the most obvious is not to include the statements as warranties, where the contract already addresses the relevant issue in a way that is acceptable to both parties, and where the benefit of a warranty is less relevant because there is already a right to terminate for (material) breach of any term.

4.1 Performance of the services in accordance with a performance standard

On most contracts, beyond the most simple ones which involve companies that are slightly more sophisticated in their own right, it is not unusual to agree that the service provider's performance standard exceeds reasonable care and skill, and to meet a standard of a 'highly' skilled and experienced provider if not the highest one. This recognises that the service provider has been selected because it is skilled and experienced but does not set the standard at a level which is too high as against the supplier's peer group.

Naturally of course there will be exceptions to this. Sometimes the service provider will be the 'best of breed' or the services are of a nature that a special level of care and attention needs to be applied to them as they are delivered, and so a position requiring the 'highest' standard will be justified.

4.2 Warranty as to fitness for purpose

Many suppliers will resist forcefully imposing a warranty as to fitness of purpose on the basis that it has provided other commitments as to the nature and quality of the service but is not in a position to guarantee that a particular objective of purpose of the customer will be achieved. Even if the purpose could be properly articulated, the service provider will likely want to argue that its approach is to deliver a service that adheres to a specification and that provides a certain set of outcomes. It cannot, however, guarantee that a particular business objective or purpose of the customer will be met.

That said, if the purpose can be carefully and relatively narrowly defined, it ought to be possible for the parties to agree that the outputs will be capable of delivering a particular purpose, at least from a usage perspective, if not from the point of view of a particular business outcome (which may be subject to influences beyond the service provider's control).

4.3 Adherence to the service levels

On the basis that the service credits are not the sole (financial) remedy in respect of a failure to achieve the service levels as agreed in connection with the relevant service level schedule, and that in association with this there is a commitment on the part of the service provider to meet or exceed the service levels, it makes little difference if there is also a warranty that the supplier shall meet or exceed the service levels. The service provider may, however, seek to insert a 'dead band' of loss arising solely as a result of service level breaches which would not give rise to separate compensation claims.

4.4 Compliance with the specification

Having an output that meets the agreed scope of requirements is clearly an important aspect of any transaction, as it inevitably goes to the very reason why the service provider is being appointed – so that the customer is provided with something that meets its requirements (albeit a set of requirements that has been validated and agreed upon by the parties). As such, it is relatively common to include a warranty with regards to compliance with specification.

The more significant negotiation point is the duration of the warranty and the extent to which the duration relates to compliance with the specification (as might be the service provider's position) or whether it talks to the 'free-fix' period, in line with the customer's expectations.

The duration will naturally depend on the specifics of the deal, and the extent to which the delivery of the relevant output forms part of a managed service or is the output of a contract to deliver a software application, solution or similar. In the latter case, a period of around 90 days is relatively common.

Accepting the service provider position that the warranty actually expires after the warranty period could leave the customer exposed in terms of its ability to seek redress in the event that the output suffers from defects after the expiry of this period. This risk may be mitigated if there is a seamless support and maintenance provision. As a minimum the customer ought, in any event, to retain the ability to revisit issues that can be traced back to the design and build, even if outside the warranty period.

4.5 Commitments to timescales

On the basis that delivery to timescales in an implementation project is likely to be a key factor for the customer, the customer will likely want to be clear as to the timeliness of the delivery responsibilities of the service provider. Most suppliers, of course, recognise this as a key part of their pledge and are committed to providing the level of service that would allow them to make this promise. The key is to identify which of the likely numerous dates the commitment should cover. In a large-scale implementation project, there will be a large number of 'milestones' which perhaps do not justify a breach of contract action if they are missed. The key is, then, to identify the key milestones that do mark genuine progress – perhaps those at the end of a phase and the final 'go live' milestone – and fix these as the definitive contractual commitments.

4.6 Warranties regarding IPR

A service provider who gives a 'full' third-party IP infringement indemnity (ie, covers any and all loss arising as a result of an actual or alleged infringement, as opposed to just losses to third parties, or court awarded damages) has some justification that it does not also need to provide a warranty with regards to third-party claims. The purpose of this warranty is, if a claim is made, to generate a breach of contract so that the customer can seek to leverage this and give itself the ability to terminate for breach, on the basis that it does not wish to remain in a contract in the situation where it has been exposed to third-party claims, either because it would not wish to contract with a counter-party that put it in that position or because its receipt of the services is suffering or is likely to suffer.

If in fact the right to terminate is specifically covered elsewhere (as a termination for breach to enable the customer to claim losses arising as a result of the termination itself), and the indemnity is as full as it should be, then perhaps the customer can form an alternative view as to the necessity of this provision.

4.7 Use of open source

Even though the real risks to using open source are better known, there remains a reluctance to a broad-brush approach within contracts to accept that it can be deployed within a solution. As such, finding and agreeing a 'one size fits all' attitude to open source approaches remains difficult. The solution is probably to identify specifically the open source components of a particular solution and to identify the relevant licences that will apply to that use, and for the service provider to warrant that no other aspects will be used. Ideally, from a customer perspective, the customer would also obtain from the service provider a warranty that the open source that would be used will not give use to any 'copy left' or 'contamination' issues.

4.8   Security

Though the situation with regards to contractual commitments on security are now heavily inter-linked with the requirements of the General Data Protection Regulation (GDPR) and how that needs to be reflected in an agreement, security provisions remain hotly negotiated as InfoSec concerns continue to be an increasing area of sensitivity and focus for boardrooms and, in this respect, the issue between a customer and a service provider tends to relate to the changing and emerging threats, as well as developments in technology and security measures over the term of a longer-term contract.

Where the agreement does specify a set of security requirements with which the customer feels comfortable, one compromise would be for this to set the applicable standard (as opposed to requiring the service provider to provide a level of security measures consistent with a more certain standard, eg, good industry practice), but that the service provider must thereafter keep abreast of threats in the market in accordance with what might be expected from a provider in that area, and for certain changes to be made to cater for these threats, perhaps with the costs to be discussed and apportioned as between the parties.

In the light of the above, it is perhaps not surprising that the warranties provisions can be one of the most heavily negotiated parts of an agreement, not least because they cover a broad set of issues. One of the biggest challenges when parties come to negotiate the warranties is the often 'standard' approach taken to them; that is, the starting point or perception that a customer needs a particular warranty because it is included in a precedent or is one that was used in a previous agreement. Similarly, approaching the negotiation by seeking to cover any and all potential variances in scope and delivery will only likely prolong the negotiations. Taking a 'painting by numbers' approach to the discussions (whether on this or another area) rather than focusing on actual and relevant requirements, will only ever result in more drawn-out discussions as the conversations meander down unnecessary paths.

The issue is additionally complicated by the possibility that the matter may be covered in other areas, such as the service level schedule or transition schedule.

The key to concluding successfully the warranties in an agreement is very likely, therefore, to be found in understanding the broader scope of the contractual terms and being specific about the nature of the requirements so that they are relevant to the deal itself.

7. Relief/excused events

1. Introduction

It is unfortunately not uncommon for things to go wrong in the context of complex outsourcing and technology delivery/implementation mandates. In many cases, this may manifest itself as things taking longer to complete or be delivered than was anticipated, such that there is slippage in respect of project milestones. In other cases, it may be that costs start to spiral beyond what was originally anticipated. In more extreme examples, there may be more fundamental questions as to whether the objectives of the project can be met at all.

In such cases, there will naturally be a tendency – if not an absolute requirement – for the parties to consider who is at fault in this regard. However, the contract may not necessarily be able to answer this question, as it depends upon an analysis of the parties' respective actions, and how the contract provisions will then be applied to them. Such forensic analysis can be difficult and subject to different interpretations.

However, an additional challenge comes up in the context of longer running engagements (and especially longer-term development projects and/or outsourcing projects); in those types of engagement, something which has gone wrong at an earlier stage of a project may only have its impact at a later stage. If, then, the customer faces a situation where it is unhappy with late or poor/non-delivery by a service provider in (for example) October and is considering making a claim, and is then told in return by the service provider that the root cause of the problems was that the customer itself had failed to perform its relevant obligations back in Q1 of the same year (or even further in the past), how can it react? It may not have all of the information, documents or personnel to hand in order to analyse properly such an argument from the service provider, such that it is faced with a greater degree of doubt as to its rights *vis-à-vis* the service provider (not least because of something known as 'the prevention principle', which is a long-standing principle under the English common law that a party claiming against another party cannot hold that other party liable for its non-performance if the claiming party had done something wrong which essentially prevented the other party from performing its obligations). Such doubt may then lead to dispute and debate, potential impasse and a potentially disastrous impact upon both the project and the relationship between the parties.

In order to help to address this mischief, it has become increasingly common to see what are usually referred to as 'relief event' or 'excused event' provisions; these initially appeared in outsource style contracts but have now become increasingly prevalent in contracts for longer running provision of services, and in particular where there are time related milestones/delivery obligations. Whatever they may be called, the essential provisions of the clause are the same, and they specifically oblige the service provider to provide contemporaneous notice to the customer of any failure on the customer's part to meet its obligations (and to in any event use all reasonable endeavours to avoid or mitigate the impact of such non-performance). The service provider will then be given proportional relief against its obligations (eg, if the effect of the customer's non-performance was to delay the service provider by five days, then the associated delivery milestones would slip by five days).

The potential sting in the tail of such a provision is that it will typically provide that the service provider will in fact only get such relief if it complies with the requirements of the clause. So, for example, if the customer is indeed in default but the contract includes a relief event clause and the service provider does not comply with it, then the service provider may still be found liable/in default under the contract's terms, even if as a matter of objective fact it was hindered or prevented by the customer from performing (see for example *David MacBrayne Limited v Atos IT Services (UK) Limited* [2018] ScotsCS CSOH 32, which reaffirmed the obligation upon a supplier to comply with the specific requirements of a notice provision if it then wanted to avail itself of defences linked to customer related deficiencies).

A typical formulation of such a clause may accordingly be as follows:

The Supplier shall only not be liable for a failure on its part to comply with any of its obligations under this Agreement (whether as to quality or timeliness of delivery or otherwise) if and to the extent that this is caused by either a Force Majeure Event or a Relief Event, and provided expressly in the case of a Relief Event that the Supplier has:

(a) *Provided notice to the Customer using the template Relief Event form attached in Schedule [X] to the Relief Event, as soon as reasonably possible upon the Supplier becoming aware of it;*

(b) *Used all reasonable efforts to avoid or mitigate the impact of the Relief Event.*

2. The customer perspective

From the customer side of the negotiation table, this provision is all about creating certainty and placing appropriate emphasis upon the project management responsibilities of the service provider. The customer will ordinarily not have visibility of what progress the service provider is (or is not) making at the detailed or technical level, and equally will not be able to predict or assess what impact any failure on its part to provide required information or inputs will have (if indeed it will have any impact at all).

Equally, the customer will be wary of the kind of scenario where progress reports during the early and mid- stages of a project are resolutely green/positive, only to then unexpectedly turn red (with associated slippages of anticipated delivery dates) when the originally agreed milestones loomed – potentially with financial consequences if they are missed. If the customer then challenges the service provider on why this is the case, it might face a snowstorm of counter allegations that the customer's own delays or defective inputs in preceding months were somehow to blame for the issues then arising. Some of this may be in the manner of blame deflection (especially in the case of more major problems, where a service provider may be worried about the potential for contract termination or litigation, and so will want to be muddying the waters as much as possible so as to make itself out to, at least, be a difficult target), but will nonetheless take time and effort (and quite probably money) to investigate and assess, and inevitably impact upon the project in the interim. Some of the allegations may even prove to be true, but may then turn out to be something that the customer was genuinely unaware of, and which it could have done something about (eg, by prevailing upon certain of its employees to turn up at workshops or provide missing information etc). This in turn breeds a sense of frustration that an avoidable problem has come to pass owing to a failure to communicate in the way that the customer would have wanted.

So, the customer will argue that it is entirely reasonable for the service provider to be obliged to actually tell it about any claimed defaults on the part of the customer which will impact upon the service provider, and to do so as soon as possible after the service provider becomes aware of them. The customer then has the practical opportunity to actually do something about them, and so avoids as much as possible of any potential impact upon the project. After all, it is the success of the project that matters most to the customer, and so it would rather know that problems are arising with the things that it is itself supposed to be doing, rather than have potential sanctions to apply in the future against the service provider. The customer may also argue that this should in any event be part and parcel of good project management on the part of the service provider, not least because the customer may not be in a position to assess what the impact of any of its own delays or defaults may have upon the services (and might act very differently if this was made known to it).

This in turn leads to the more contentious aspect of these types of clauses, that is, what happens if the service provider doesn't provide notification to the customer (either at all, or contemporaneously when becoming aware of the customer's delayed or non-performance)? From a customer view point, there has to be some kind of consequence of such non-compliance, as otherwise there will be little point in having the clause in the first place. For example, if the service provider knows that even if it doesn't notify the customer of the delays or non-performances in question it will still be able to get relief for any resulting delays etc regarding its own obligations, either by way of the contract provisions or by virtue of the prevention principle as discussed above. There is then little incentive for it to serve such relief notices which might prove to be inflammatory to the relationship with the customer and cause unpleasant conversations with customer stakeholders that the supplier would prefer to avoid having. If, however, the service provider knows that it has to serve a notice in the format and in accordance with the process mandated by the contract, if it wants to guard against being held liable for non-performance against the contract in any event, then it is far more likely in practice to do so. The customer is bolstered in this view by arguing that – at least in normal circumstances – it is the service provider who will have the professional project managers and the information at hand to note what the status of the project is and to assess the impact of any delays by either party, and accordingly it is most reasonable for the supplier to bear the risk of failing to undertake such project management in the way that the customer wants (ie, with full transparency).

3.   The service provider perspective

The service provider view starts with the simple notion that it feels unfair for it to be potentially held liable for a failure on the part of the customer to meet its own obligations. After all, such obligations will often have been negotiated at some length and then clearly set out in the contract, such that there should be no excuse for the customer to both be aware of them, or to not be responsible for policing its own resources so as to deliver against them. While the service provider may in good faith monitor the overall project and try to point out to the customer when it is in default, it would appear penal to then apply all of the results of such non-performance against the supplier, were it to fail to do so.

The service provider may further argue that it will not necessarily be apparent to it that a delay or non-performance by the customer will actually have an impact, or to assess what such impact will be. For example, if a customer representative fails to turn up to a key scoping meeting to provide inputs, will that simply result in the same number of days of delay as is the time between the scheduled meeting and when they do in fact turn up? Or will this be greater because the information that they then impart has a significant impact on work that had been done in the meantime and now needs to be reworked?

If the form to be completed appears to be in the form of an overly legalistic and/or aggressive claim style form, the service provider may also argue that adopting such a procedure may ultimately be to the detriment of the project (and the relationship of the parties as a whole). This may lead to a degree of finger pointing and blame assignment from an early stage, when in fact it may be better for both parties to be working more collaboratively together so as to make as much progress as is reasonably possible and as quickly as possible, regardless of whether or not one party or the other is doing 100% of the things that were originally expected of it. Perish the thought, but the required contents of some relief notice templates look as if they might need to be completed by litigation-minded lawyers, such that both parties may be involving legal counsel far earlier in the project lifecycle than might usually, or ideally, be the case, leading them each respectively to start to 'take positions' on the causes of problems rather than constructively resolving them (and so actually creating disputes rather than avoiding them, as is the stated intention of such clauses).

The service provider may also note that while it may not have an issue with taking the steps which it is reasonable for it to do in terms of seeking to avoid or mitigate the impact of a relief event, this will not necessarily be without cost. As such actions are only becoming necessary by reason of the customer's original defaults, the service provider will likely want to ensure that it will in any event be entitled to recover the costs of such actions.

4.   Potential solutions

There is considerable truth in the argument that the drafting of some relief event/excused event clauses that we have seen have become too aggressive, and appear to be more in the form of setting traps for the service provider to fall into. For example, by setting absolute time limits on when written notifications have to be given, often measured in numbers of hours rather than days; by requiring detailed and highly prescriptive forms which have to be sent in writing rather than by email to senior executives and copied to legal teams; or providing that notifications should be made as soon as the service provider either was 'or ought to have been' aware of the relevant defaults by the customer. It is as if the original point of having the process (ie, to avoid disputes and to help the project remain on track) has been forgotten, and instead they are used more as a shield to protect the customer, come what may.

That said, in order for the process to work, there is an absolute need for the customer to know what it is that it needs to sort out, and at a time when it is still practical for it to be able to do something about it. That in turn necessitates contemporaneous notification, and for there to be some kind of consequence for the service provider if it fails to do so (ie, by losing the ability to latter use the customer's non-performance of its obligations as a defence versus its own late or non-performance).

However, there are some modifications to the process which can be made in order to make the process work better in practice and to avoid some of the downsides from the service provider perspective. In particular, one can adjust the process by making the notification of a relief event into more of an operational/commercial issue, as opposed to one which requires the service of a more adversarial and legal notice. For example, one could provide that there be in a regular governance meeting a specific agenda item as to whether there are any relief events to be notified, such that there can be no doubt that the customer is then aware of them (which is the first aim of the overall process), they are being notified in a timely way (so long as the governance meetings are themselves reasonably frequent, eg, weekly or fortnightly), and they appear more as a normal project matter rather than something which requires the involvement of lawyers or which should be immediately triggering alarm bells. In this case it is not so much what you say, but how you are saying it.

It would also be reasonable in principle for the service provider to be able to recover the costs of the mitigating steps it may take to avoid the impact of the relief event (as such costs would not have arisen in the event that the customer had done what it was supposed to have done, and would not have been possible for the service provider to anticipate or price for upon the commencement of the contract). However, this should be subject to the costs of such steps being subject to approval by the customer, on the basis that the customer may for example prefer to suffer the impact of a delay to the timetable as opposed to the challenge to its budget that would be entailed by the service provider instead finding a costly way of circumventing the customer's own delays or resourcing issues.

A slightly trickier issue is the cost of any wider impact upon the service provider (eg, if it cannot prevent the customer's default from impacting upon the project, but then suffers a loss or cost as a result). Such losses may again be difficult to anticipate, but obvious examples might include having to keep resources available for longer than originally anticipated, and without them being able to undertake worthwhile work in the meantime. Simply allowing the service provider to automatically invoice for such costs would actually put the service provider into a better position than the customer would be in, *vis-à-vis* defaults or delays by the service provider (as the customer would then have to bring a formal claim against the service provider in order to recover them). On balance, however, the customer may consider this to be a reasonable *quid pro quo*, if coupled with a provision which makes the service provider's relief preconditional upon it following the relief event process, and in the light of other potential incentive provisions that may in any event be included in the contract in relation to the service provider's late or poor performance (such as liquidated damages for delays in meeting milestones, or service credits accrued in relation to missed service levels).

8. Intellectual property provisions

1. **Introduction**

   Intellectual property (IP) rights lie at the very core of most, if not all, technology-related transactions. At the end of the day, they will be the determinants of what the customer is actually getting in return for its payment, and what the service provider will be committing to provide. They will equally be crucial to many elements of the business rationale for the deal, in terms of the scope of usage which both parties may seek to have in respect of the outputs from the project, both during its initial term and thereafter.

   When talking about IP rights, there are many different types of rights which may arise, including trademarks and service marks, rights in respect of semi-conductor topographies, design rights and database rights. However, the two most important IP rights for the purposes of the negotiation of the majority of technology contracts will be copyright (put simply, the right not to have work/materials copied or used by anyone else without the owner's permission), and patents (which at an equally high level can be described as the grant of a monopoly right in the manner of expression of a particular idea). Patent rights are the more powerful right given the prohibition upon anyone else doing the same thing (even if they reached the same end result by different means and without access to the right holders' own materials) and as a result are subject to an assessment and registration process (which is done on a geographic basis) and are time limited. They are also more limited in terms of what they can be granted in relation to (eg, they are generally – in the United Kingdom and European Union at least – not granted in respect of software *per se* unless forming part of a bigger end-to- end process or invention). A more general analysis of the nature of IP rights and their associated requirements is however beyond the scope of this book.

   The question of ownership of IP rights is sometimes seen as a black-and-white/binary debate, where one party owns the rights and the other does not (and by implication therefore has no rights in respect of the underlying materials at all). However, the reality is that there is a spectrum of possibilities, and where the parties will end up in relation to them will very much depend upon their bargaining leverage and also their commercial imperatives. At a high level, the range and sequence of options might be summarised as follows:

- the customer owns all rights, the service provider has no continuing or separate rights of use;
- the customer owns all rights, the service provider has limited licence rights (potentially subject to customer consent or restrictions on use with customer competitors or for designated lock-in periods, or linked to commercial arrangements whereby the service provider has to share a percentage of any revenues earned from use of such IP rights with other clients in future with the customer);
- the customer owns all rights, the service provider has more extensive licence rights with fewer restrictions;
- the customer owns all rights, the service provider has licence rights which are drafted as widely as possible and which are tantamount to ownership in all/most material respects (eg, including the right to modify or adapt, assign, sublicence to third parties etc);
- they have joint ownership (more on this, below);
- the service provider owns all rights, but the customer is granted wide licence rights which are tantamount to ownership and which extend in perpetuity;
- the service provider owns all rights, but the customer is granted extensive licence rights with few restrictions;
- the service provider owns all rights, with the customer having only limited licence rights (potentially only limited to the period of time when the service provider is actively engaged in providing the underlying services to the customer); and
- the service provider owns all rights, and the customer has no independent usage rights at all (eg, it receives a service as an output, but all tangible work products or modifications etc created as a result of the services remain vested in the service provider).

Where the parties land in relation to the options above will be heavily dependent upon the nature of the deal, and the underlying commercials. For a software as a service/SaaS deal, for example, the service provider may well argue that all the customer receives is a service which it can access remotely, and so everything else which the service provider creates or develops in connection with the services will remain vested in it. At the other end of the scale where the customer has commissioned the bespoke development of a new application with the express intent that it will deliver it a competitive edge in the market place or will be capable of being commercialised with other third parties, it will understandably be expecting to then own the IP rights in that application to the exclusion of anyone else (including the service provider), so as to ensure that no one else is in an immediate position to compete with them.

Before proceeding to consider the respective positions of the parties, we will expand on the issue of joint ownership. In some cases, it may be tempting from a lay person's perspective at least to default to the option of joint ownership, in the belief that this frees both parties to do what they want with the work products in question. While this would be true in terms of their internal use of such work products, the default position would then be that any use of such work products with any third parties, including any sublicensing or sale of such work products, would then require the consent of both joint owners, so giving each of them a right of veto over the potential commercial activities of the other. This may of course be the intention of the parties, but it will more likely not be the case. In such circumstances, the parties should consider how to moderate this position through their contractual agreement (eg, by specifying up front what each of them will be pre-authorised to do with the jointly owned materials, without having to first obtain consent from the other party, nor offer them any commercial return associated with such use).

2. The customer perspective

Very often, the customer position is reflected in a very simple statement: "If I paid to have it developed, then I should own it."

Even the hardest of customers will readily concede that this should not extend to the pre-existing materials of the service provider which may be supplied alongside any work products or which may be incorporated within them, but the customer will want as wide as possible a licence right in respect of such pre-existing elements, namely one which is perpetual, non-terminable, transferable, worldwide, sublicensable and royalty free.

Otherwise, the customer may argue that seeing as the materials in question would only have come into being based on what the customer paid the service provider to do, it then should be the party who is able to enjoy the fruits of those particular labours, both in terms of its own business use and potentially also any further exploitation of them which may be possible in future with third parties. For example, if it turns out that newly developed software could be used by other affiliates within the customer's corporate group, it will want to be able to freely provide it to them. Equally, if it transpires that there is interest from third parties in such software, the customer will want to retain the right to licence the software to them and so reap the rewards of any associated licence fees.

In other contexts, the assertion of ownership rights may be more by way of a defensive measure, and so as to avoid a potential lock-in scenario with a given service provider. For example, in a long-term service provision arrangement such as an outsourcing contract, many new processes, interfaces, applications etc may be developed, not all of which will have been able to have been either listed or even contemplated at the time that the contract was first entered into. There is a risk, then, that if the customer does not own the IP rights in such materials (or, at the very least, maintain a very wide and royalty free licence right in relation to them), its ability to transition away to a different supplier in future may be severely hindered, if not stymied altogether. For example, this could happen if the outgoing service provider says that any use of such materials in which it then owns the relevant IP rights will cease as at the point in time when it stops providing the relevant services to the customer. This, therefore, leaves the customer potentially without the means of obtaining such services at all (if its replacement supplier does not have immediately available alternative products, software or other materials ready to replace them, without the need for a lengthy integration or implementation programme). Or, alternatively, it could leave the customer with an unpleasant surprise of having to bear an additional cost that it had not anticipated (either in the form of the outgoing service provider demanding an ongoing licence fee, or the new supplier charging more than would otherwise have been the case in order to implement its own replacement solutions/products).

The customer will, in any event, not want to leave the contract silent in this regard. This is because, under English law at least (other jurisdictions, including States in the United States, differ in this respect), if the contract does not specify anything to the contrary, then ownership of new IP rights (and most particularly copyright) will vest in the author, which in this context will most likely mean the service provider. This can frequently come as something of a shock to customers who signed up to deals without proper legal advice. We had one example of a client organisation who had in effect funded its service provider's research and development (R&D)

activities for a new software product for over three years, only to find that at the end of such engagement it had no formal rights at all to the fruits of all of those labours. Also, the service provider proposed to charge them a considerable licence fee for any continued use of them. As an aside, there may then be legal arguments available as to the extent of what kind of implied licence might be created, but plainly it would be in the interests of both parties to ensure that the contract is clear from the outset and so as to avoid the hassle and cost of having to run such arguments in future.

Where the customer is expecting to acquire ownership of new materials, it will likely want the scope of the grant of rights to be as wide as possible. This may, for example, be crafted as a grant of all IP rights (howsoever and wherever arising) in all jurisdictions in the world, arising out of or in connection with the relevant agreement or provision of the relevant services. The customer may build on to that an obligation upon the service provider to do all such things and sign all such documents as may be necessary to perfect that grant of rights.

There is then the question of what happens if for any reason someone comes out of the woodwork to challenge whether the service provider did, in fact, have the ability to grant the rights that it purported to grant (either in terms of the ability to pass on title, or to grant a licence in the terms that it purported to do). For example, a past client of the service provider may argue that it had in the past paid the service provider to develop the materials or product in question and had retained ownership of the resulting IP rights under the terms of their own contract with the service provider, such that the service provider was not then entitled or able to provide them to anyone else. The customer may therefore seek:

- an express warranty from the service provider that it has the ability, consents and authorisations necessary to pass the title and grant the licences that it commits to do under the terms of the relevant contract; and
- an indemnity from the service provider (usually outside the normal liability limits – see Chapter 11) in respect of all losses, costs or damages which the customer incurs by reason of a breach of such warranty and/or any third-party claim of infringement of their IP rights.

3. The service provider perspective

The service provider comes at the issue of IP rights from a different angle. Again, the exact scope of their argument will vary depending upon the nature of the underlying services/products, but very often it will be based upon one or more of the following key arguments.

- *The balance of interests.* While the customer is focused upon its wider business (which the service provider and its products or services will simply be enabling or supporting), what the service provider will have created will likely be at the heart of what they are all about. As such, they will argue that the balance of need in terms of ownership and future exploitation lies in their favour.

- *Commercials.* The service provider will frequently argue that its pricing is predicated upon it being able to continually develop its offerings, based on the work and developments done for its clients. As such, if the customer were to seek to impose some different position upon it such that it would not then have the ability to make such free use of such work and developments with other clients in future, then the service provider would have to either decline to do the work at all or, at the very least, uplift its charges so as to reflect the loss of usage that it would have in future.

- *History of development.* As an adjunct to the previous point, the service provider may point to the fact that its current services and/or products will likely be the result of work that it has done not just within its own R&D labs and facilities, but also with other of its clients in the past. Indeed, it is precisely that kind of past experience and development which may have enabled the service provider to put forward its overall offer to the customer, and which may in turn then have led the customer to select the service provider. The service provider will then argue that it would be illogical to then agree with the customer IP right provisions which would then effectively preclude it from continuing with such a path with future clients.

- *Future development.* Where the newly created materials are an adjunct to or a further development to a core solution of the service provider, and the customer envisages making use of such solution over a longer-term period (eg, in relation to a major software application or cloud solution), there may be an adverse economic consequence for the customer if it refuses to allow the service provider to own the IP rights in the newly created materials. This is because the service provider will then be precluded from incorporating such materials within its core product set, and so as to be covered within its standard support/service offering. That may then constrain the further development that the service provider may itself be willing to invest in relation to such materials (and which the customer may otherwise have benefited from). It may also result in higher costs for the customer in the shorter term (as the service provider may say that it will have to charge more in order to maintain a group of service personnel who are familiar with the customer's own divergent version of its core solution, separately from its normal service or support team).

Even if the service provider does agree to cede ownership of certain IP rights to the customer, it will likely want to be very specific in this regard. Accordingly, the grant may be limited to only certain specifically listed/identified deliverables, as opposed to just anything newly created which arises in connection with the agreement.

When it comes to warranties and indemnification, the service provider will obviously be keen to limit its exposure as much as possible. As such, it may argue that it should not have to grant a warranty if it is in any event separately offering up a form of indemnification protection, and then seek to limit such indemnification obligation:

- to only valid third-party claims (ie, only ones which are proven or accepted as a basis for a settlement agreed to by the service provider);
- to just those amounts paid to such third parties, either in the form of damages following a court judgment or by way of a settlement agreed to by the service provider (and so excluding the customer's internal costs, which the service provider will argue it cannot control and so should not be responsible for);
- so as to exclude claims which result from materials provided by the customer, the customer's specifications or directions, use other than as expressly directed or agreed by the service provider, usage with other third-party materials, or from alterations or modifications not made by the service provider itself; and
- so as to oblige the customer to accept any reworked or modified products which would avoid the impact of the claim, or to cease using the infringing materials if necessary (potentially with a right to then have a refund of any associated fees for such materials, less a reasonable adjustment to reflect for use actually made prior to the date of the claim).

The service provider may then provide that such indemnity obligations are to be its 'sole and exclusive' liability, so as to provide for a boundary for its obligations in respect of IP related matters.

4.   Potential solutions

The solution to these arguments concerning IP rights will vary tremendously depending on the nature of the arrangement in question.

For cloud services deals, for example, it will likely be the case that the customer does not receive 'work products' *per se*, and instead simply receives an output by way of the online services, whatever they may be. In those cases, the service provider will have a stronger argument in favour of retaining all licence rights in newly developed materials.

Similarly for on-premise software licence arrangements, there may be little point in the customer arguing for ownership of developments to the core software product, if it would not be able to use such new developments in isolation from the main product in any event (and particularly if it does not have a perpetual licence for such product, as opposed to a term or subscription based one).

For outsourcing transactions, the customer will have a stronger argument for at least having broad continuing licence rights, and so as to avoid the poison pill/lock-in issue as referenced above.

In contrast, for consulting style inputs or engagements where the end products are more unique to the customer and its requirements, the customer's argument for retaining overall ownership will be much stronger.

In relation to all of the above, the parties should in any event consider what we have said at the outset of this chapter with respect to the spectrum of potential options *vis-à-vis* both ownership and licence rights, such that even if one party asserts a stronger claim to ownership of any newly created IP rights, it may still be willing to grant a broad scope of licence to the other party. Equally, it may be necessary to distinguish different types of work products, such that ownership in them will vest in different parties.

The impact for the service provider of not having either absolute ownership of IP rights or the wider scope of ongoing licence rights to the related materials may also be offset by including appropriate contract provisions regarding ongoing use of 'know how', namely the knowledge of the service provider's personnel as to what they had done for the particular customer, and how they had done it. This would then allow the service provider to still sell its expertise and experience to future clients, but on the basis that they would then have to recreate the relevant materials or products from scratch for such clients. In practice, they should then be able to complete the relevant development work faster and cheaper than was the case for the original customer, but the customer should at least then have a period of time before its potential competitors will be able to enjoy the equivalent benefits of whatever the service provider had developed for the customer.

It will also normally be reasonable to place limits on the scope of any ongoing licence rights that the customer may have in relation to embedded elements of pre-existing service provider materials. So, it could be provided that while the customer can have licensed right to use, such embedded elements must not be separately extracted from the work products or deliverables that they have been provided with. As a *quid pro quo*, the customer should then ensure that such licence is worded as being transferable, if and to the extent that the customer in future transfers ownership of the deliverable or work product in question (eg, as part of a business sale).

One other point that should now be called out specifically in the context of the negotiation of IP related provisions is the treatment to be given to projects involving the application of robotic process automation or forms of artificial intelligence (AI). The application of AI tools is becoming ever more widespread in relation to various forms of technology engagements, and raises some interesting new challenges. To take but one (more legalistic) example, in many jurisdictions the question as to ownership of the first instance of any IP as may be created is determined by reference to a human author (or set of co-authors). The question then is: how is this to be determined when new works are created by software programmes, or combinations of software programmes operating in concert with each other, and with little (if any) additional human interaction? As current legislation will frequently not provide a clear answer to this question, the contract must take centre stage.

The interests of the parties will need to be carefully balanced in this regard; the service provider will want to preserve its rights in whatever AI solution it is utilising (if and to the extent that it is its own proprietary solution, as opposed to one licensed from some other third party), given the increasing importance that such solutions play in the delivery of technology-based services. However, the customer will also be wary about what will happen with the taught version of any AI tool, that is, the data layer which represents what the software has been able to learn and so deliver, which will often be a representation of weeks or months of effort and inputs from the customer's own personnel. The ownership and future use of such data can be absolutely critical. In one case we dealt with, an organisation came very close to signing its own death warrant in terms of what seemed to be a relatively straight-forward AI-based SaaS agreement, in that the project involved them spending a huge amount of time in working with a well known supplier and their AI tool to teach that tool how to do certain manual processes which were fundamental to that organisation's business, but on the basis that the supplier's contract terms would then have vested ownership of the final work product/data sets in the supplier. So, allowing the supplier to simply launch a new SaaS service as from the end of the relevant subscription term to compete directly with the customer's business. It is likely therefore that while the customer will be willing to allow the supplier to continue to own any modifications to the core AI software itself, it will want to continue to assert ownership/exclusive use of the data sets which represent what it has then learned specifically about the customer's business processes (and so as to potentially map such data sets across to alternative AI tools used by other suppliers, in the future).

9. Data protection liabilities

1. **Introduction**

Data protection and privacy has been an increasingly hot topic over the years. Appreciation has gradually grown as to the value and importance of personal data, and the means by which it can be exploited and monetised, sometimes for valuable and laudable purposes, but often for reasons which are less well appreciated and which may not bear much public scrutiny (the Cambridge Analytica affair in the United Kingdom being one particular example).

It is not, therefore, much of an exaggeration to say that data is 'the New Oil' when it comes to its role in modern business, and while not all of this data will necessarily be personal data, much of it will be. This is particularly so when we bear in mind the breadth of the definition of what constitutes 'personal' data, that is, data by which a living individual can be identified, either on its own or by reason of being combined with other information in the possession or control of the party in question. Ensuring that there are appropriate controls on its use and processing therefore becomes key.

At the same time, there has been an equally significant shift in the levels of concern regarding cyber security and data breach events. These have gone from isolated occurrences to near daily occurrences, and with major financial and reputational impacts for those involved. There is a genuine sense of 'there but for the grace of God go I', as organisations big and small fall victim to ever more sophisticated cyber assaults, and even those organisations with traditionally the highest levels of security (such as government bodies and financial institutions) find themselves facing the consequences of unauthorised disclosures of personal data.

Sitting above all of this is the change in the legislative landscape. In the European Union, this is embodied by the General Data Protection Regulation (popularly referred to as GDPR), which not only reshaped the nature and scale of data processing related obligations, but also changed to entire liability related landscape by switching up the quantum of potential fines to 2% or even 4%

of global turnover of the relevant corporate group. To put this in context, the maximum fine that could previously have been levied by the Information Commissioner's Office in the United Kingdom was just £500,000. In that context, data protection breaches can be said to have been shifted from a slap on the wrist to a more existential threat, such that a service provider could find that a sufficiently serious data breach or data processing scandal with a single client could be sufficient to push it into insolvency.

This has collectively given rise to an interesting divergence of approaches from customers and service providers in terms of their negotiation of data protection related liabilities, and a near unprecedented degree of flux in terms of the drafting one now sees in relation to the associated contract terms.

2.   The customer perspective

The customer angle regarding personal data will likely be a prescriptive one. A typical customer focused clause would:

- oblige the service provider to process personal data (or indeed customer data in the round) only and strictly as required to provide the services and for no other purpose;
- restrict the processing of personal data to agreed locations and jurisdictions (and with mandatory imposition of EU Model Terms *vis-à-vis* any processing that is proposed to be undertaken outside of the European Union, such as in back office service locations in India);
- require the service provider to in all circumstances comply with applicable laws and regulations in relation to its handling of customer data (which takes on added significance now that the GDPR imposes direct obligations upon a service provider as a data processor, while the pre-GDPR regime had focused more on the imposition of obligations upon the customer as ultimate data controller);
- impose specific IT and physical security requirements (eg, as may be set out in a detailed security schedule to the contract, or by reference to the customer's own security policy), but often with an overlay of overriding obligations upon the service provider to maintain appropriate technical safeguards. These safeguards to be linked in with references to what is perceived at the time to be in line with the 'state of the art' (using the same terminology one sees in the provisions of the GDPR); and
- require the service provider to take on unlimited liabilities in relation to any losses, claims or liabilities as may result from its breach of any of its data related obligations (both *vis-à-vis*

personal data and more generally). Such liabilities would then not only encompass the customer's own internal losses (eg, costs incurred in seeking to reconstitute lost or corrupted data from data backup tapes), but also external claims such as fines imposed by data protection/privacy regulators, or claims brought by end clients of the customer or individual data subjects (whether on their own account or as part of a data related class action).

The customer's perspective in this regard will be that as the risk profile associated with the protection and processing of data has increased, so must the focus of the service provider in ensuring that data is handled appropriately and protected from third parties. In the mind of the customer, the best way to get the service provider's undivided attention to these obligations is to not only make them prescriptive, but to also take them outside the normal limits of liability.

3. The service provider perspective

The service provider community, perhaps not surprisingly, takes a different view.

Going back a few years, it would not perhaps have been uncommon to see service providers accepting relatively widely drafted data protection related responsibilities, and also having them linked to unlimited liability provisions. However, this was largely because while the service provider would appreciate the sensitivity of dealing with personal data, it could also be comforted by the fact that the actual risk profile was relatively low.

For all of the reasons described above, this perspective has now changed. Instead, the service provider will be concerned that data-heavy engagements could have a high risk both in terms of the possibility of defective processing/corruption and also in terms of being targeted by third parties set upon obtaining unauthorised access to such data. Moreover, if issues then arise, the service provider faces not just the possibility of internal costs and losses of the customer, but also potential third-party claims from data subjects and data protection regulators. In the latter case, in the light of the changes introduced by GDPR, such claims could also be brought directly against the service provider in its role as service provider, as opposed to being 'flowed down' through the contract terms via the customer, in its role as data controller. While the service provider can still look to limit its liabilities with regard to its customer by way of the contract provisions, it clearly cannot avoid the risk of such direct claims, in any event.

With that risk profile in mind, the supply-side community has initially moved in the opposite direction to the buy-side one. So, initially a shift from accepting unlimited liability for data protection related claims, through to imposing a cap on such claims or even trying to exclude liability for them altogether (eg, via an exclusion of liability for all losses arising from loss of or corruption to data) can be seen. They have also picked up the fact that simply restricting or limiting liability in respect of the specific data protection clauses in the contract may not be enough, in terms of protecting their interests. In given circumstances, it might be possible also to characterise a personal data related incident as also being a breach of confidentiality (if it involves a third party gaining unauthorised access to the data concerned), a breach of applicable law or regulations (if there is a breach of the requirements of GDPR or any equivalent local legislation), or a failure to adhere to security related obligations. If any of those provisions would separately allow the customer to assert a claim for uncapped losses (as would traditionally be the case for breaches of confidentiality, for example), then the service provider may remain exposed to the kinds of doomsday liabilities that it is seeking to avoid.

Service providers will often also go further and seek to introduce additional provisions so as to reduce the likelihood of them being in a position of being in breach of contract in the first place. Examples of drafting we have seen in this regard include:

- prohibitions upon the customer providing any personal data in connection with the provision of the services;
- express warranties (and potentially indemnities) from the customer regarding its ability to provide any personal data for the purposes envisaged in respect of the provision of the services; and
- obtaining acceptance from the customer that a documented set of security related arrangements will, as between the parties, be treated as being adequate for the purposes of protecting the data to be handled in connection with the services, and such that if there are then any changes to be made to such arrangements, they will need to be agreed (and paid for) by way of the contractual change control provisions.

4.   Potential solutions

As at the time of writing, we are relatively new to the world of GDPR in the European Union, and with other jurisdictions still in the process of implementing their own data privacy and protection regimes (eg, California). It is perhaps, therefore, premature to be talking of any new market standard as having yet developed, let alone hypothesise as to where such standard should be set.

However, given the challenges which have been created, it is fair to say that there a great deal of attention has been placed upon the data related provisions in the technology contracts which are currently being negotiated out in the market. Accordingly, negotiators have been identifying some potential solutions which are being seen with increasing frequency.

When it comes to the central question as to the quantum of potential liability that the service provider may take on, the focus in this regard appears to be on the creation of a form of separate (or 'super') cap which will be triggered in relation to data protection related claims. The logic to such an approach would be that the service provider would want to recognise the customer's concerns as to the nature and potential seriousness of the underlying issues and potential losses, but would not want to be exposed to unlimited liability and so would be willing to put some more 'skin in the game' by way of an increased cap, instead.

With such an approach, there remain several variables to be managed, as follows.

- *Will it be restricted to just breaches of the data protection clauses?* As noted previously, service providers are nervous about being exposed to unlimited liabilities 'by the back door' in the event that a default in respect of personal data might be argued to also trigger liability under a different part of the contract, which is not then subject to the limits of liability (eg, the confidentiality obligations). The application of the super cap may therefore be extended to all claims and losses regarding personal data, regardless of which provision of the contract is said to have been breached. A further area of potential negotiation in this regard may then be whether any other categories of loss may be given the same treatment. We have, for example, seen drafting which extends the ambit of the super cap approach beyond just claims regarding personal data, but also more widely to claims regarding breaches of IT security obligations, or the imposition of fines or sanctions arising from breaches of applicable law or regulation.
- *The quantum of the super cap.* Clearly, there is the scope for some considerable debate between the parties in this regard, and we have seen a tremendous degree of variation in terms of the end points which we have seen negotiated

in recent times. Sometimes the super cap is expressed as a simple figure (eg, in USD, Euro, Pound sterling etc), with no direct linkage to the level of spend with the service provider on the relevant project. In other cases, it is expressed in a similar way to how the primary limit of liability is drafted (which will most often be by way of setting a percentage of the charges paid or payable to the service provider), but then setting that percentage at a higher level than such primary limit of liability (eg, if the primary liability cap was set at 150% of relevant charges, then the super cap might be set at 250%, etc, with both percentages then no doubt being subject to avid debate). In certain business process outsourcing and similar projects that we have seen, the relevant service providers have instead tried to take a more mathematical/ reasoned approach by creating a cap which is linked in some way to the number of customer records or files that are handled in relation to the project (on the basis of an argument that this is then a reasonable way of assessing the size of the risk/exposure, albeit that there is as yet no clear indication that this is an approach that the relevant regulators would adhere to or adopt).

- *The interplay between the super cap and the primary cap.* This is in fact a lot more complex than might at first appear. If, for example, we were to say that there was a 'normal' liability cap set at 100% of relevant charges, and a super cap of 300% of relevant charges, there would remain a number of potential interpretations (at least unless the contract drafters had been sufficiently clear), as follows.

  - The super cap could operate as an 'uplift' to the normal limits of liability, such that if a personal data related claim were to arise, the claimant could bring a claim of up to 300% of the charges, but in doing so would first be exhausting the 'normal' limit of liability, before being able to then access the enhanced limits agreed to in the contract. In such circumstances, if a future claim were then to be made for a non-personal data related breach (assuming that the contract had in any event continued beyond the resolution of the first claim) and if the original data claim had involved a liability of more than 100% of the relevant charges, the claimant may then have nothing left in the liability 'pot' that it would be able to recover. Equally, if earlier claims had already been made which had reduced the amount of the normal liability cap which was then still available, the balance left for the claimant to recover might be lessened accordingly.

- The super cap could alternatively sit on top of the normal limits of liability. In this scenario, the claimant would be able to claim for the amount of the super cap (300%), plus the amount of the normal liability cap (100%), such that its total recovery for the personal data related claim could be 400% of the relevant charges.

- As a third option, the super cap could sit in parallel to the normal limits of liability, but on the basis that it is then an exclusive remedy in relation to personal data related claims. Under this model, the claimant could recover up to the 300% of relevant charges cap for the personal data related losses, but would not at the same time be able to access the additional 100% of relevant charges liability pot under the normal liability cap. Such normal liability cap would however remain available to it in relation to any non-personal data related defaults as might then arise in future.

As such, different interpretations could give rise to a very different quantum of recovery in practice, it will obviously be essential that the parties negotiating the contract are crystal clear in their drafting, in terms of the outcome that they intend that the contract should embody.

Moving on then to other areas of potential contention and where solutions need to be found, there is the question of who has responsibility for defining the technical and organisational measures which are necessary to protect personal data from unauthorised disclosure. In this regard, it may be helpful to draw a distinction between the systems/operations in question. Where the systems are those of the customer itself (eg, in the context of an IT outsourcing engagement), then it may be more reasonable to expect the customer to specify (or at least sign off on) the specific security measures to be undertaken, given that this is what it would have had to do on its own account, prior to the commencement of the outsourced services. If, however, the infrastructure in question is within the control and design discretion of the service provider (as would be the case with a cloud-based service), then it would be more reasonable for the burden to fall upon the service provider. The service provider may, however, still reasonably ask to be informed of the broad nature of any personal data that it may be asked to process in the course of the provision of the services and/or of any changes to such types of data during the course of the contract term, so that it can assure itself that the measures that it has in place remain appropriate for the types of data in question.

10. Benchmarking in outsourcing transactions

1. Introduction

Benchmarking is the process whereby a customer of outsourced services is able to compare, and therefore 'benchmark' the pricing and performance of their outsourced service provider against those offered by others. Although such provisions could potentially be applied to other types of technology services as well (at least to the extent that such services are provided across elongated periods of time), in practice they tend to be limited to outsourcing transactions (and this chapter proceeds on that basis).

1.1 Why would the customer need to include such provisions in its outsourcing contract?

Benchmarking is one of a number of contractual levers which enable a customer, concerned that activities which were previously provided in-house, and which are now being provided by a third party, to know that it is continuing to get a fair deal. Mid- and high-value outsourcing arrangements usually are long term, and will require a transition period to move the relevant services from the customer or a previous incumbent, and then a number of years for the customer to realise the benefits of receiving a service from an expert provider and for the service provider to earn a sensible return.

So, locked into a multi-year agreement, how does the customer know if its deal is still competitively priced and high quality? And conversely, from the service provider perspective, how can the service provider agree to be benchmarked if it has effectively just gone through that process in order to win the deal? The answer is a balance of fair and reasonable provisions which are sufficient to give the customer comfort, without being unduly burdensome for the service provider.

High-level objectives may not be enough to achieve this and sourcing agreements usually contain a variety of mechanisms and requirements to formalise the aim. Benchmarking and continuous improvement provisions are two such mechanisms. Essentially benchmarking is about testing competitiveness (of the agreement price, performance and, sometimes, the type of services). It involves an independent third party, the benchmarker. Whereas continuous performance is concerned solely with identifying an implementing service improvements.

Both mechanisms can vary in their implementation. For example, they might lead to 'change control' (requiring agreement of both parties) or they might be hardwired into the agreement such that obligations to increase productivity, efficiency, reduce pricing or improve service levels are automatic.

1.2   To benchmark or not

In large outsourcing deals, benchmarking is common and even considered best practice from the customer perspective. But is it always worthwhile? Large, complex deals may simply be too expensive to benchmark, and the rewards not match the expense and disruption. Equally, other shorter-term deals may not be worth benchmarking (as the customer will instead simply do a re-tendering exercise), and more unusual types of outsourcing may be difficult to benchmark, if there are then likely to be fewer other deals to compare against (and for which the data is actually available).

Nonetheless, depending on the financial model that underpins the outsourcing contract it may be a useful tool if certain factors are considered.

- *Is it a hollow right?* Will a party really seek to invoke the process?
- *What is the amount of effort required?* Can the process be run efficiently and can the contract provisions be agreed quickly?
- *Is the contract long enough?* The longer the contract, the more likely that it will be appropriate to benchmark. It is only usually worth having the right to benchmark in contracts of five years duration or more.
- *What is the charging model?* A fixed-price agreement might not be suitable because the benchmarking has essentially been undertaken before entering into the contract itself. Of course, even if the price is fixed, it may still be sensible to benchmark service levels or technical specifications.

1.3   Who can undertake the benchmark?

A key issue for both parties is to get comfortable with the identity of the benchmarker. How independent and qualified must the benchmarker be for both parties to be happy with their work, to respect the outcome, and to avoid any conflict of interest in the results?

Depending upon the negotiation leverage of the parties, a customer will often seek to have sole discretion to appoint the benchmarker; the negotiated position, however, is more likely to have the benchmarker taken from a pre-agreed list. That will allay a service provider's concerns that the benchmarker is somehow in the pocket of the customer or an organisation which will not have access to sufficient data to undertake a proper comparison and benchmark process. The worst-case is to leave the identity of the benchmarker to agreement between the parties at the time. This is problematic because the process can be frustrated through lack of agreement (ie the service provider could effectively 'veto' the process by simply refusing to agree to any benchmarker proposed by the customer).

1.4 Who and what will be compared against?
Comparing like with like is essential for the process to feel fair and this is not as simple as it seems: often service provider solutions will be bundled, cross-subsidised and made up of a multiplicity of home grown and third-party solution elements which may make it difficult to perform a true comparison. So, for example, a negotiated clause may be to identify the 'headings' of service which can be benchmarked as a whole. In a recent example we have seen the 'services' broken down into 'networks', 'help desk', 'service ops' and so forth. It was agreed by the parties in this case that each of those headings would be benchmarked as a whole.

1.5 How involved can the parties be?
Whether the benchmarking is a wholly independent, desktop exercise, or a hands-on process more akin to an audit, including submissions by both parties (or something in between), will need to be clarified.

1.6 What does 'good' look like?
Furthermore, the parties will need to be clear as to whether 'good' means 'good value', 'market leading', 'upper-quartile' from a representative population or some other, preferably objective criteria so as to avoid debate as to the outcome. Customers will normally aim for upper quartile, while service providers will try to aim for mean or median.

1.7 What happens next?

The success of a benchmarking exercise ultimately lives or dies by its consequences. It may be that the outcomes are used for an executive review, or to force a renegotiation, or in some cases to automatically require the service provider to change its solution or pricing. Whatever the desired outcome, it must be clearly understood and set out in the outsourcing contract at the point of signature to avoid debate and dispute later on.

2. The customer perspective

2.1 Required provision or negotiation chip?

Taking into account the considerations above, customer perspectives on benchmarking range from must-have to highly tradeable. In the public sector for example, where value for money concepts are writ large in both standard contract terms, procurement law and policy, benchmarking is seen as common practice. By contrast, in the private sector the exercise of running a competitive outsourcing process will itself often satisfy the customer's needs with regard to market testing, meaning that the concept is either traded in negotiation entirely, or watered down.

2.2 Let's be clear, this is a customer-centric concept

Benchmarking can be seen as a hostile act of the customer, used to achieve price reductions. Unsurprisingly this view is more likely to be held where the benchmarker is retained to act for the customer. This is an approach which can lead to negotiations and even disputes (eg, as to the reliability of the data or the basis on which comparisons have been made).

2.3 How often should the right be exercised?

Customers usually wish to retain the right to specify when a benchmarking exercise is to be conducted. Benchmarking is, however, rarely appropriate during a transition/transformation period. After this, it is typically available annually for commodity services and perhaps once every two to three years for more complex or bespoke services. That said, particular projects can justify a different approach.

2.4 Approach to the comparison

Any benchmarking comparison must be fair, comparing like with like. The benchmarker should have a database of information about deals. For standard services (eg, desktop support) there should be sufficient data available for the comparison exercise. However, more individual projects are less easy to benchmark. From the customer perspective, the customer will seek to benchmark all or part of the services. They do this essentially to slice-and-dice the scope of services so as to cross-check that each substantive element of the contracted scope represents a good deal.

3. The service provider perspective

3.1 When can a service provider welcome a benchmarking process?
The process can be more acceptable to a service provider where the benchmarker is selected from an agreed pool of independent organisations and the service provider is allowed to comment upon the findings of an 'interim benchmark report'. That way the process is more controlled from the service provider perspective, and the risk of more perverse or mode sided findings is reduced.

3.2 How often should the right be exercised?
A service provider will require sufficient prior notice and will look to limit the number of times a benchmarking exercise can be undertaken (and the period of time between each exercise). Further, a service provider will want to be given a chance for the service provision to bed-down. As such, and as noted above, it is not uncommon to negotiate a lock-out period and limitation to frequency.

For example, in a five year outsourcing agreement with a six month transition period, a service provider may be prepared to welcome the benchmark concept provided that there is no benchmarking during transition, nor for the first two years of the agreement, and then the benchmarking is only undertaken once during the final years of the agreement.

3.3 Approach to the comparison
From the service provider perspective, it is critical that the comparison must be fair, comparing like with like. In particular, service providers will resist customer attempts to slice-and-dice the scope of services and often will only agree to a benchmark of the services as a whole (on the basis that it would be unfair to require a price reduction regarding service tower A, if the service provider is providing really pro-customer pricing for service towers B, C and D, etc). In doing so, it is sometimes possible for the service provider to neuter the impact of the benchmarking right completely because there is simply

nothing identical to compare against, or insufficient comparators. The service provider may therefore require that there be a minimum number of comparator organisations, and/or a minimum number of other projects to be included in the benchmark process.

4.   Potential solutions

4.1   Sensible representative samples

It is advisable to agree at the outset of the exercise how many comparables constitute a representative sample to ensure that any statistical analysis is meaningful.

The service provider will understandably want to narrow the scope of a valid comparable (ie, to the same services or at least those which are substantially similar). However, if the scope is too specific there is a real risk that a representative sample will never be achieved. Both parties should appreciate the legal issues that may arise where, because of the lack of adequate aggregation of the data, sensitive information about other companies' pricing can be deduced. This risk is heightened where the service provider is part of a consolidated market with few players. As a result, most parties will use one of the larger benchmarking organisations which has sufficient data to ensure a meaningful comparison is achieved and will be aware of the competition law sensitivities. Additionally, a service provider will typically impose obligations of confidentiality upon the benchmarker and ensure that any benchmarking reports, and other benchmarker communications, are confidential.

4.2   Setting the benchmark

The whole exercise is about competitiveness, but the customer needs to decide where it wishes to be positioned against the market. The cheapest deal may be a lossmaking transaction for the particular service provider and so sourcing agreements often require charges to fall within the top quartile (ie, the lowest 25% of the range) for other similar agreements for similar services. If the customer insists on being in the top decile (ie, the cheapest 10%) the risk of the analysis being distorted by outlying unreliable data is much greater and the service provider will look for additional protection.

4.3   Implementing the benchmarker's recommendations

There is no point negotiating-in a benchmarking provision without clear agreement as to what will happen if the benchmarker concludes that the charges are too high, or service levels too low.

There is a very real possibility that benchmarker's final report may conclude that the price and/or service specification or service levels are not in line with the market (or the particular target threshold which has been agreed). The customer will want to ensure that price can only go down, not up. For the service provider, the issue will be the extent to which price reductions and/or service level improvements can be imposed on it. The service provider will, of course, add a risk premium if it considers that it is exposed to mandatory price reductions.

The agreement should also provide for a fixed point in time by which the benchmarker's recommendations should be implemented (as it may take the service provider some time to adjust its delivery model so as to mitigate the impact of any charge reductions it may be obliged to apply). The service provider may also want to negotiate a right to terminate rather than accept the obligations created by the benchmarker's proposals in all circumstances. This 'get out' for the service provider becomes more important where the process is adversarial. From the customer's perspective a 'get out' for the service provider is rarely a satisfactory outcome and it undermines the cost and effort of conducting a benchmarking exercise if it cannot be implemented afterwards, or can only be implemented by terminating the contract and incurring the cost (and risk) or then transitioning across to a new supplier.

In more detail, a negotiated solution often establishes controls around the benchmarking outcomes. These may include the following.

- A 'deadband' before adjustments apply, ie a percentage variance which the parties find acceptable. For example, this could be +/- 5%, but the deadband needs to be related to the elements of the services being benchmarked. So, while a 5% variance in charges for an element of the services might be acceptable, a 5% variance in service level is likely not to be acceptable.
- Whether there should be a maximum adjustment that can be required to be applied. This arises when (for example, in public sector outsourcing) the profit margin is known. A service provider will not wish for a benchmarking to make the contract unprofitable and for the service provider to be locked-into a bad deal.
- Whether the service provider can decline to implement the benchmarker's recommendations should be considered. It might be agreed that forcing a service provider to implement

is not in either parties' interests but then what should be the outcome? Often the logical outcome of an adverse benchmarking report, and failure to implement is contract termination, without payment of a fee (because this is not a 'termination for convenience').

4.5   Who pays for the benchmarking?

In practice, the parties usually agree to share the costs of benchmarking. While the customer may hope all of the costs will be borne by the service provider if the benchmarker concludes that the charges are too high, the service provider will counter that the customer should foot the bill if the benchmarker concludes that the charges are 'market'.

In fact, this debate is relatively pointless because the customer will pay for the agreed share of the benchmarking costs anyway because the service provider will factor this into its charges.

There are, therefore, many issues to consider in drafting effective benchmarking obligations both on a micro level (clause by clause) and on a macro level (by asking what the clauses are trying to achieve, what other mechanisms in the agreement will achieve). These are uncomfortable provisions for a service provider, who will typically seek to keep them broad unless it is allowed to share in the benefits. If this is not the case then it is often down to the customer to push for these mechanisms to be included in an enforceable and realistic way.

11. Setting limits of liability

1.   Introduction

1.1   Why do we limit liability in contracts?

All business deals need to find a suitable balance between risk and reward from the perspectives of both the customer and service provider. An unlimited exposure is rarely acceptable to a sophisticated organisation (although, oddly, certain template agreements which are silent on the liability position for their counterparty and which are a trap for the unwary can still be found). Balancing liability through forms of limitation makes a deal tolerable to an organisation, able to be signed-off by relevant stakeholders and represents a suitable position whereby the 'reward' means that the deal is worth entering into, and the 'risk' is manageable (with rights and remedies in the event that issues arise).

With some notable and important exceptions, commercial entities are largely free to agree between themselves how to apportion this risk and to limit their respective liability to each other. This can take varied forms from the complete exclusion of liability for specific types of loss to requiring claims to be made within a specific time frame.

There are various considerations frequently used to limit a party's liability under a contract. These include the following.

- *Symmetry.* Should both the service provider and customer have equal and opposite limits, or is it appropriate that the regimes be deliberately asymmetrical? Two parties in a collaboration arrangement may have equal reasons for entering into the contract, whereas in an outsourcing arrangement it is normal for the customer to seek protections which are higher than those offered to the service provider.
- *Liquidated.* Should the provisions in the contract limiting liability be tied to a set sum, or derived using a method? There is no right answer to this question, but a customer will often seek a cap which is set by reference to a multiple of the contract charges, (if the liability limit is calculated on an annual

basis by reference to spend), whereas other customers prefer the certainty of knowing that they have the potential to seek redress of a set amount, eg, 'up to £x'. For some organisations this hardwiring of liability limit is preferred for internal sign-off purposes.

- *Application.* Should the cap chosen apply on a per year basis, or per event basis, or (as certain service providers are increasingly seeking to agree) on an aggregate basis to cover the entire term of a contract? A 'term basis' limit brings its own challenges: if there is a claim in Year 2 of a six-year contract, using up 75% of the available liability regime, are the parties happy to continue with the contract for another four years with only 25% left?
- *Different limits for different circumstances.* Should liability be treated as a single concept or sub-divided into types of claim and loss? In a typical outsourcing arrangement, the heads of possible loss will be sub-divided into a number of concepts (loss of data, damage to property, security breach, breach of confidentiality, poor performance and so forth) and the parties will need to agree the appropriate treatment for each. (See Chapters 9, 12 and 13 for discussion of excluded liabilities, unlimited losses and data protection liability.)
- *Treatment.* A triangulation of thinking is needed: capped verses uncapped verses unlimited. For each possible loss the following questions have to be asked. Firstly, should the liability be capped or uncapped? In other words, should it be without financial limit? Here, imagine a 'vertical axis' of £s, whereby, for example, property loss could be capped to an agreeable sum, depending upon whether the performance of the services could put buildings at risk. Next, should it be unlimited? In other words, should it be without limit to types of loss recoverable? Here, imagine a 'horizontal axis' for the imaginary graph. This refers to the 'width' of possible claims, by which is meant direct, or even indirect losses can be stated in the contract to be recoverable. So, for example, while the limit of liability for breach of confidentiality might be uncapped (vertically), it might be limited to direct losses only (horizontally). The basis that recovery should be available should not be forgotten here (ie, via a damages claim or on an indemnity basis).
- *The clause in context.* Should the liability clause trump all others or be subject to certain other clauses? For example, it would be a normal request from a service provider to ensure that payments it might have to make under a service credit regime are offset against claims for damages regarding the

same event, but some may go further and argue that all service credit payments over the term should erode the sums available under the general damages cap (which would be far less palatable for the customer).

- *The unexcludables.* Should the liability provisions be distinct from certain circumstances which the parties agree cannot be limited? It is normal to recite that parties cannot exclude or limit liability for certain implied warranties (for instance, any clause which purports to supply goods without the right to do so), death or personal injury caused by their, or their employees, negligence and fraud and fraudulent misrepresentation. However, each contract will have its own context and so for a customer who is particularly concerned with security, the security provisions of the contract might also be grouped together with the unexcludables. Similarly, where the purpose of a contract is for the sharing and exploitation of valuable intellectual property (IP), IP infringement might also be treated in the same way.

1.2 What should the limit be?

As discussed below, service providers and customers will perform a similar analysis, but from a different perspective, in order to reach an agreed liability position. While discussion and negotiation will come down to the specific wording of clauses, the liability limit will be seen in the context of the outsourcing transaction itself. As such, there are many input considerations which both parties will keep in mind in order to reach a mutually satisfactory outcome, including the following.

- *Nature of services.* Different types of services will give rise to different risk profiles, for example, the risk and reward profile pertaining to a straight 'lift and shift' of an existing scope of services from an incumbent to a new provider is substantially different to the risks and rewards that arise when the supplier is required to transform processes, technology and culture, or where it is proposing to provide a commodity-style cloud-based service. 'Transformation' projects can be particularly risky as that will usually mean that the affected user community (staff, customers and so forth) will need to get used to doing something differently, and even if 'different' is 'better' there is still a very apparent risk of 'tissue-rejection' by the customer organisation. A common reason for refusal may then be "it's not how we have always done this" (rather than a non-compliance with an actual contract requirement). That is a risk for the service provider. No matter how fantastic and modern the service provider's solution might be, the tissue-rejection risk will mean that it will be more cautious, because performing the services is going to be more difficult. That will play into the liability limit setting, because the customer may seek to blame failure for its organisation to realise the benefits of the new systems and processes upon the service provider.

- *Pricing.* A contract where there is significant upfront or early payment presents a very different profile to a contract where payments are received for 'proper' performance and subject to a performance regime. An annual basis calculation for liability cap will not work well for the former model, and, as discussed below, a service provider will need to know that its potential risk matches its revenue and profit, whereas a customer will need to know that it could seek recompense up to the right amount during the term of the contract.

- *Governance.* A good relationship throughout the negotiation and contract finalisation process, coupled with a sensible contract management approach with clear communications, expected (good) behaviours and a 'fix-first, settle-later' mantra will cast the possible liability set out in the liability clause in a different light. From the customer's perspective the customer may need to have all the appropriate rights in its contracts (for regulatory or perceived common practice reasons), but it may be very recalcitrant to actually exercise those rights. Similarly, a service provider with a long-term relationship viewpoint may be able to get comfortable with challenging liability wording if it feels that it will be unlikely to ever be in a dispute which would require the clause to be called upon.

- *Exclusions.* As discussed in more detail in Chapter 12, a sensible list of elements for which liability is always excluded is essential to help to create the balance of risk and reward.

1.3   A model for a liability clause

Contracts vary as to their treatment, and certainly in terms of their wording of a liability clause, but common themes can be derived. These are set out below so as to examine the treatment of each element from both the customer and service provider's perspective to derive the appropriate limit of liability.

Common practice, backed by case law reasons to ensure enforceability, mean that a liability clause is typically drafted in a number of discrete parts.

- *Unlimited liability statements.* Typically, a liability clause will start with a list of items for which liability will not be limited. That aids interpretation and helps to ensure that the clauses which follow are more likely to be held enforceable (in a B2B context). This list of items will include death and personal injury caused by negligence, fraud or fraudulent misrepresentation, breach of implied terms as to title and 'any liability to the extent it cannot be limited or excluded by law'.

- *Contract-specific unlimited liability statements.* Depending upon the nature of the agreement, these might include reference to concepts which are set out as indemnities elsewhere in the agreement, such as: damage to physical property, loss of data, security requirements, confidentiality, breach of data protection provisions and so forth. A customer-friendly agreement will include this list and make it clear that the service provider's liability under those indemnities is unlimited. Equally, it is often typical to see that the customer's liability for Transfer of Undertakings (Protection of Employment) Regulations 2006 (TUPE) and employment indemnities given elsewhere in the agreement are also expressed as unlimited.

- *Financial and other limits.* In the context of the unlimited elements, the parties then negotiate suitable financial limits. These are usually split between a limit for physical property loss or damage (if that concept is not already captured above in the unlimiteds), a statement regarding the interplay between the liquidated damage and/or service credit cap and the general liability cap (usually to clarify whether such payments erode the liability cap, or are in addition to potential damages), and finally, the financial caps for general losses themselves (for both parties).

- *Liability limits and payment obligations.* A good liability clause will also make clear whether payment of the charges by the customer is independent from, or rather erodes, any damages which might be payable under the general financial loss limit.

- *Consequential losses.* Next, the clause will specify those things which the parties have agreed are too remote to be recoverable. That might include loss of profit or goodwill but the list will depend upon the context of the agreement.

- *Deemed direct losses.* Increasingly, it is becoming more and more common to follow the list of consequential, and therefore unrecoverable types of loss with a list of what the parties agree would be recoverable. This is the subject of much debate and negotiation (eg, in certain contracts where there has been an outsourcing of a regulated function of the customer, there is a risk of fines from the regulator which the customer will be keen to ensure is listed as a deemed direct loss and therefore recoverable from the supplier; by contrast, for a standard licence or software as a service (SaaS) offering, the service provider will likely be far less willing to accept such a position.

So, in the context of all of the considerations set out above, the question to ask is: what is the typical view of the customer and service provider to setting an acceptable liability limit?

2. The customer perspective

The customer may be taking a risk seeking to find a service provider who will take on one of its functions and provide a better service than it can provide itself, at an acceptable cost. Alternatively, it may be procuring a service which is intrinsic to its business operations. So, if things go wrong, the customer will need to:

- unwind the relationship;
- take back responsibility for the function (if it is able to);
- find another provider (particularly if the customer has now lost the ability to self-provide); and/or
- retrain the user community again, losing credibility and support for the change process.

Expressed in those terms, a mere 'pay back' liability limit is clearly not sufficient. As such the customer will be looking for 'refund-plus'.

In more detail and taking the model for a liability clause structure set out above as a guide, a strong customer liability perspective will look like this.

- *Unlimiteds.* This will be a full list of those items unexcludable by law and it will express inclusion of elements which apply to the customer's business and sector. If IP is a heavy element of the agreement then the customer will expect the service provider to stand behind IP ownership entirely and so IP infringement loss will be unlimited (and recoverable) on an indemnity basis. If the agreement is data-heavy, and/or featuring data identifying people then both data security and data protection losses will also be included.
- *Contract specific elements.* The customer should check whether there are customer-specific needs which, by convention, are

stated to be unlimited. For example, in the security sector or where the customer has particularly key physical assets, in which case property damage might also be unlimited.

- *Financial.*
  - *Property.* If such losses are not unlimited (see above), then the customer will argue that the service provider can cover a large proportion of them by way of normal insurance arrangements. Negotiations will discuss how an error or breach by the service provider's employees might risk the destruction of a customer's key property and the rebuild cost so as to justify this large number.
  - *General losses.* This is a multiple of the payments the customer is making. It is typically expressed on an annual basis. If a comparison is made between the standard templates of large banks, public sector bodies and other customers with considerable leverage, a typical limit will be at least 150% of the annual charges.
- *Liability and payment.* The customer will make it clear that any payments made should be refundable, if the deliverables which they relate to are ultimately rejected.
- *Consequential losses.* The customer will likely agree to the normal statement regarding the irrecoverability of consequential losses but will ensure that this does not include contract-specific concerns (for example, if the contract has been concluded with the stated aim of finding savings then 'savings' should not feature in the list of consequential losses). In addition, this list of consequential losses will be stated to be expressly subject to the list of deemed direct losses, below.
- *Deemed direct losses.* This will ideally be a long list from the customer's perspective, including wasted expenditure, wasted management time, the cost of reprocurement, any fines imposed by a regulator, bank charges imposed, compensation paid to a third party, anticipated savings, costs of conducting indemnity claims, cost of idle time of staff, costs incurred by the customer's group, loss of revenue, the cost of taking emergency measures, the cost of replacing lost, stolen or damaged goods and the costs of dealing with a data breach (which itself may include express reference to legal costs, engagement of monitoring staff to ensure that the breach does not reoccur, and the costs associated with notification of affected persons).

3.   The service provider perspective

The service provider is in business to earn profit for itself, and, if listed, for its shareholders. By ensuring that its reputation is held in high regard, and by winning more and more deals in its chosen focus sectors, the service provider can demonstrate that it is a market leader and a true expert in its field.

The stronger that expertise becomes, the stronger the negotiation leverage that the service provider can wield. As such, for certain technology transactions, the service provider's negotiation strength will be stronger than that of the customer. This means that often a supplier of an ERP system or enterprise cloud solution, for example, will only deal on its own terms and conditions, and will only entertain minor modifications to those terms, often captured separately in an addendum, to match the bespoke needs of the deal at hand.

In liability terms, this means that service providers of this sort are looking through the other end of the telescope from the customer. The world looks very different and so their view of what is market standard does not match the customer's view. A deal will need to be worth the while for the service provider. There is no point agreeing to a liability regime which would wipe out the service provider's entire expected profit, and worse.

Of course, there is no uniform supplier view, but a typical liability position is illustrated below. As between competing suppliers in the technology space there is a palpable range of views, from those who are more risk averse to those able to walk towards a customer's preferred position. It is difficult to generalise, but those service providers with core technology underpinning their services tend to take a stronger view on their 'must have' liability and contractual provisions. By comparison, more established system integrators can often look less attractive by virtue of their robust contractual positions compared to newer entrants who are able to take a riskier contractual position (relying instead on client management to avoid dispute) so as to win market share.

In more detail and taking the model for a liability clause structure set out above as a guide, a strong supplier liability perspective will look like this.

- *Unlimiteds.* This is the list limited to those items unexcludable by law.
- *Contract specific elements.* Here there is a reversal of the customer-expected position such that the service provider makes it clear that any loss or damage caused by the customer relating the supplier IP is recoverable on an unlimited indemnity basis.

- *Financial.*
  - *Property*. There is no separate head of loss. This is covered by the general losses below.
  - *General losses*. These are limited to a maximum of the contract value, either on a yearly basis, or (increasingly) to an entire term basis. That might be expressed as a 100% plus limit, but how that works should be checked. A common service provider approach is to state that the cap is, for example, 150% of annual charges, but to then be applicable for the term of the agreement; in such event the amount seems high, but is set by reference to fees accruing in a single year, and yet also is then intended to apply to the entire term of the agreement.
- *Liability and payment*. In addition, there should be a clear statement that the customer is still obliged to pay the contracted charges, and these are not reduced by a damages claim.
- *Consequential losses*. Here, there will be the normal statement regarding the unrecoverability of consequential losses, with no deemed direct losses.
- *Deemed direct losses*. This does not apply, in the preferred model of the service provider. There will be no such deemed direct loss, and everything as to whether a loss is direct or indirect will be left in the hands of the court (or chosen dispute resolution forum, if not the courts).

4. Potential solutions

At the outset of negotiations, the mark-up returned by one party on another's standard positions can seem insurmountable. The liability clause is a prime example of this, and is often one of the last elements of a contract to be resolved. This is because both parties are seeking the right balance of risk and reward; a contract that makes sense, achieves both of their aims and provides comfort should things go wrong.

As such, to arrive at sensible and mutually agreeable liability limits requires a wider perspective. That perspective needs to take into account many elements, and often, this can only be done once those elements are agreed. For example, the parties will want to be clear on the following:

- the charges are clear and agreed;
- the expected level of service is achievable (and the penalties for poor performance are clear and either fully compensatory or in addition to general damages claims);

- the service provider will need to be completely clear as to the customer's technical and organisational environment (and if not, capture dependencies and assumptions in a way which afford time, money or performance relief);
- there is a clear meeting of minds on the customer's requirements and the service provider's solution; and
- the other elements of the liability regime are understood, ie, quite how extensive the list of elements which are unlimited is and how many concepts are recoverable on an indemnity basis.

There is also a trend for the list of indemnified losses in IT and outsourcing contracts to be getting longer and longer. To start with, one needs to assess what the more traditional view may be as to the benefit that an indemnity clause may provide, as opposed to a pure damages claim. The main differences (at least under English law) are perceived to be the following:

- with an indemnity claim, there is no need to show fault or negligence, it suffices to show that the trigger for the indemnity has occurred;
- there may be an ability to recover all loss which causally flows from such trigger event, no matter how remote or indirect it may seem to have been; and
- there is no requirement for the indemnified party to show that it has mitigated or sought to reduce or minimise its loss.

As such, the parties negotiating the liability clause will need also to consider the basis of recovery and if that basis is by indemnity rather than a pure damages claim then the indemnity may have the effect of increasing the quantum of any potential claim. It is also a misconception to believe that limits of liability set out in the contract automatically do not apply to loss simply because it is expressed to be recoverable on an indemnified basis. The drafting is very important here; indemnified loss might, for example, be accidentally excluded from the cap on liability if the cap is expressed as applying to any and all damages payable under the agreement.

In more detail, and taking the model for a liability clause structure set out above as a guide, a middle ground may look like this.

- *Unlimiteds.* This is a list limited to those items unexcludable by law, and those elements which are key to the nature of the contract and the customer, eg security only.
- *Contract specific elements.* There should be a balanced clause making clear, for example, that the customer is concerned

with security and the service provider is concerned with the protection of its intellectual property rights, such that liability for both is unlimited (or caught by a super cap of some sort). It is becoming increasingly normal for there to be a super cap for data protection breach and losses arising. (This is discussed in more detail in Chapter 9.) A mutual recognition that either party's liability for TUPE and staff issues is unlimited and recoverable on an indemnity basis.

- *Financial.*
  - *Property.* There should be a separate head of loss, set by reference to possible property reinstatement but mitigated by an assessment of the likelihood of that occurrence such that the limit does not fully reflect the full value of a rebuild.
  - *General losses.* These should be expressed to be on a yearly basis, at 100%, or slightly more, or a set figure (whichever is the greater). Detail can be added to work out a suitable limit for the first year of the agreement where the charges might be lower.
  - In the alternative, the parties may agree a full-term limit, based on a multiple of one year's charges with a provision stating that if a claim arises which uses up more than 50% of the available limit then the customer can ask the service provider to replenish the liability pot, or seek termination for convenience (not for cause).
- *Liability and payment.* A clear statement that the customer is still obliged to pay the contracted charges is needed, and these are not reduced by a damages claim, provided that the services relating to those charges have been performed.
- *Consequential losses.* This refers to the normal statement regarding the unrecoverability of indirect consequential losses. This should be accompanied by the proviso that the exclusion above does not preclude the recovery of direct losses, often with an illustration to state that wasted expenditure will be deemed recoverable.
- *Deemed direct losses.* These are covered above.

In summary, the liability provisions are a source of consternation and provide detailed consideration of the nastier elements of a contractual relationship: when things go wrong. As such, they take time, and need to be agreed once both parties feel that they have a clear view of the entire contractual landscape.

The drafting of the clauses and the setting of limits is fraught with traps for the unwary (be that a missing liability cap, meaning that a party's liability is unlimited, or falling foul of caselaw regarding direct and indirect loss of profits).

Nonetheless, if taken in a structured way the issues can be considered calmly, and if discussed with colleagues within the customer or service provider team by reference to real-world examples and likely events, then the true risk profile can be understood and successfully negotiated with the other party.

12. Excluded liabilities

1. Introduction

Regardless of how high or low the main liability cap has been set (see Chapter 11), many technology related contracts will set out an additional list of types of loss which will not be claimable in any event, regardless of whether they can be said to have been caused by a default of one of the parties to the contract.

It is important to note at the outset in this regard that not all losses will necessarily be claimable as a matter of law, if the contract is otherwise silent on this point, under English law and in the event of a claim for damages in respect of a contractual breach, the test remains as set out in the famous case of *Hadley v Baxendale* ([1854] 9 Ex 341). The test is in essence a test of foreseeability, that is, so that the loss will only be recoverable if it was a direct result of the breach, or the type of loss was of a type in the contemplation of the parties as at the point that the contract was entered into. The loss must be foreseeable not merely as being possible, but as being 'not unlikely'. *Hadley v Baxendale* splits this into two heads of claimable loss, being 'first limb' loss which was a direct and natural result of the breach in the sense of happening 'in the ordinary course of things'; and the 'second limb' as being loss which was communicated to the defendant or otherwise known to the parties as being a likely consequence of breach (as judged at the time that the contract was entered into). Note, however, that other jurisdictions may not have the same understanding of what indirect loss includes and indeed may not recognise it as a concept at all.

In less legalistic terms, a way of looking at this would be to say that the first limb is what is objectively foreseeable (ie, what someone unconnected with the contract would have thought would be likely loss arising from a breach of the contract in question), whereas the second limb would be what was subjectively foreseeable (ie, foreseeable by the parties to the contract on the basis of their own individual knowledge). The first limb is what is often termed 'direct' loss whereas the second limb is what is referred to as 'indirect' or 'consequential' loss. The significance of those terms will become clearer in the sections below.

Any loss which does not fall into either of the two limbs of *Hadley v Baxendale* as described above would not then be recoverable under a contract breach claim, on the basis of being too remote.

With that background context, it is open to the parties to the contract to adjust the position so as to make additional losses claimable (eg, by setting liability on a indemnity basis, such that all loss can then be claimable, so long as a causal link can be established to the trigger event for the indemnity in question) or, for the purposes of this chapter, to specify certain types of loss that will not be claimable.

2. The customer perspective

The customer will most often be the party bringing a claim (as the service provider will generally – albeit not always – have the greater proportion of obligations to fulfil, and will therefore have the greater proportion of risk of failing to do so). As such, it would be in the customer's interests to have no adjustments to the rules of claimable losses as set out above, or indeed to adjust the position so as to express its right to claim loss as being on an indemnity basis so as to actually expand its ability to recover its losses. We do, for example, from time to time see contract drafting which extends the scope of indemnities beyond the usual suspects *vis-à-vis* breaches of intellectual property (IP) rights and Transfer of Undertakings (Protection of Employment) Regulations 2006 (TUPE) related liabilities, so as to also cover breaches of all warranties or representations in the contract (which would then be likely to be wide enough to cover the vast majority of service defaults by the service provider, assuming that the service provider has given a warranty to exercise reasonable care and skill in the delivery of its services, as would be usual in a standard service delivery/warranty clause).

It would, however, in any event be very much market standard for most technology related contracts for there to be an exclusion of indirect and/or consequential losses. The basis for this is somewhat lost in the mists of time, as it is certainly a commercial/drafting decision and varies the normal rules on recoverability of contractual damages, as explained in the introduction to this chapter. As has been explained above, indirect/consequential loss would ordinarily be claimable in a contract breach action as being within the second limb of *Hadley v Baxendale*, but a general acceptance has developed in the market that the balance of risk and reward in technology contracts at least should be set on the basis that only the direct/'ordinarily occurring' loss should be claimable.

The customer will however usually want this to be the only head of excluded loss. Its argument will be that the fair balance of risk and reward is otherwise already addressed by way of the acceptance of whatever limit of liability has otherwise been set (ie, such that the customer runs the risk that it will have to bear the burden of any loss it suffers which is in excess of the cap, and believes it would be unfair then for it also to have to bear any loss within such cap, simply because it falls within the scope of what could be said to be an arbitrary exclusion). The customer's argument will therefore be that it has in effect already offered up a compromise to the service provider's risk position by agreeing to the exclusion of indirect losses (as would have been claimable as a matter of common law) and so should not have to agree to any further exclusions.

3. The service provider perspective

The service provider's position on exclusions is an extension of its position regarding the liability provisions in general, namely that they should reflect the balance of risk and reward that the service provider is willing to accept in the context of the project and services in question. As such, the service provider will usually want to exclude as many heads of specific types of loss as possible, so as to reduce its overall risk profile.

Additional candidates for absolute exclusions (and the service provider-side rationales for them) include what follows below.

3.1 Indirect/consequential losses

The service provider perspective in respect of indirect/consequential losses is that they should not be liable for such losses as they are not part of the 'ordinary course' of what they as an organisation would expect to be exposed to (in terms of potential losses), given the nature of the services in question. Namely, they are losses which are by their nature more specific to the individual project and customer and so are harder to predict in advance as part of the service provider's overall risk analysis.

3.2 Loss of profit/revenue

The service provider view in this regard is that it is providing a service or product for the customer to use in the context of the customer's business. It is willing to accept the cost of replacing that service or product with one that works in the event that its supply of them proves to be defective, but is not willing to act as a form of insurance policy for the customer in terms of the business benefit that the customer had hoped or expected to achieve or gain by reason of such use. The service provider will argue in this regard that it does not share in the upside for the customer in this regard (eg, it does not get paid any additional amounts in the event that the customer is able to achieve even greater business benefits than it might have anticipated) and so should not bear the business risk in terms of any reduced revenue or profits. The thinking of the service provider in this regard will be driven by the likelihood that if such losses were to be claimable, then in the event of any serious interruptions or issues with the relevant services, it would be far more likely that any claim by the customer would then be up to the very top end of any applicable limits of liability.

3.3 Loss of anticipated savings/benefits

A similar argument applies in relation to the exclusion of anticipated savings or other benefits. The service provider's position in this regard will be that while there may be a hope or even an expectation that the provision of the relevant services or goods will enable the customer to achieve savings of costs in terms of its business operations, the service provider is not guaranteeing that this will in fact be the case and so will not accept liability if it proves not to be the case. Underpinning this is also a desire to avoid a difficult evidential burden and likely argument as to causation, for example, as to whether the service provider's defaults did actually lead to a loss of savings or benefits which would definitely otherwise have been realised.

3.4 Loss of goodwill/reputation

The primary driver for the desire to exclude any loss associated with loss of goodwill or reputation is the difficulty associated with trying to calculate it, in a financial sense. If, for example, the provider of a software solution suffers a major bug which brings a mobile operator's network down (as for example happened in the United Kingdom in the tail end of 2018), there will clearly be a significant degree of end-user dissatisfaction (which will be primarily aimed at the customer rather than the service provider, even if the service provider's software was actually the cause of the problem). However, accurately relating that to a financial loss is not straightforward. Would it, for example, be based on a drop in share price? (But what then happens if the share price recovers?) Might it be based on the loss of revenue associated with end customers who then either cancel or refuse to renew their contracts with the customer on the basis of what has happened? (But how then can it be proved that this was as a sole or even direct result of this particular outage?) Or could the argument be based around any reduction in the volume of new business during the following period, based upon a comparison with previous periods? This would be based on an argument that any drop off will be likely to be due to a deterioration in the public's perspective of the customer's service offering. As can be seen, each of these potential lines of attack have clear challenges and would likely be both difficult and therefore also expensive to try to defend/rebut, and that cost could be used as a lever by the customer to extract a larger overall settlement from the service provider, in the event of a dispute arising. By excluding such loss absolutely, the service provider accordingly removes that threat.

3.5 Loss or corruption of data

The service provider position on data (which is recognised as being of ever greater importance and value to the operations of businesses of all sectors) is that the customer should remain responsible for making appropriate backups of all data that is provided to its various suppliers, such that if there were to be any issues with those suppliers, it will be able to rapidly and easily recover any impacted data and so avoid or at least substantially mitigate any data related losses. On that basis, the service provider will say, it should not have any liability linked to the customer's potential failure to have done so.

3.6 Amounts payable to third parties

The service provider's justification for this exclusion will be that it wants its liability to be limited to the party it has contracted with, that is, the customer itself. The service provider's position will be that it will not be able to foresee or control what the potential knock-on impact will be on the customer's third-party connections, other suppliers and clients. For example, the service provider may point to the customer's ability to agree to onerous contract terms which may create too much of a dependency upon the service provider's products or services. It may be possible for the supplier to argue that such losses would in any event fall outside the *Hadley v Baxendale* recoverability tests, but the service provider will prefer to have the issue put beyond doubt so as to avoid having to argue the point in court, and so have the losses identified as being excluded from the get-go.

4. Potential solutions

4.1 Indirect/consequential loss

It is fair to say at the outset that – at least under English law contracts and those subject to common law jurisdictions which have a similar notion of what 'indirect loss' consists of – there is not usually any leeway in negotiations as to the inclusion of an exclusion of indirect and consequential loss. This is the case despite the fact that many people mistakenly assume that such losses are those which are too remote to be claimable, as opposed to those which fall within the second limb of the *Hadley v Baxendale* test, as explained above.

However, a very common compromise position that we have seen employed is to have a list of heads of loss that the parties agree will be deemed to be direct losses and therefore claimable (ie, such that the parties are in effect pre-agreeing that they will not raise any arguments in future litigation that losses falling with such heads would be otherwise caught by the exclusion of indirect and consequential losses). Depending on the nature of the services and project involved, such deemed direct losses may include:

- wasted internal administrative/management time;
- costs of conducting a reprocurement exercise; or
- additional costs of procuring replacement products or services (over and above what was expected to be incurred in any event).

It would be fair to say in this regard there has been a tendency in practice for such lists of claimable losses to become ever longer. The parties should be mindful in this regard not to let the list become so long and widely drafted such that the intended exclusion of indirect and consequential losses becomes effectively meaningless. It should also be remembered that while this approach would make the listed heads of loss claimable as a starting point, the claimant party would still have the burden of proof of establishing breach, causation and quantum, and also to show that they had appropriately mitigated their losses (ie, the fact that such losses are being pre-agreed as being claimable does not then obviate the normal rules of contractual damages).

It is also worth noting that contracts will usually be drafted on the basis that indirect losses can be claimed in cases where loss is recoverable on an indemnity basis rather than by way of a simple damages claim, although this is a position which can be changed depending on the actual wording in the contract. Great care must accordingly be taken in drafting the relevant indemnity provisions.

4.2 Loss of profit/revenue
It is fair to say that an absolute exclusion of loss of profit has for a long time been the market standard in most if not all technology

related services contracts. Indeed, until the case of *British Sugar Plc v NEI Power Projects Ltd* ([1998] 87 BLR 42) there appeared to be a working assumption amongst many lawyers that loss of profit would automatically be seen as a form of indirect loss (and so caught by the usually uncontested exclusion of indirect and consequential losses), and the ruling in that case that loss of profit could be recovered by the plaintiff insofar as it could be said to constitute direct loss had many lawyers running to update their precedents so as to expressly exclude loss of profit, regardless of whether it was a direct or indirect loss (to varying degrees of success, as a series of other court decisions such as *Pegler v Wang* [2000] BLR 218 were to show).

Larger service providers with significant bargaining power tend to stick to this position (and certainly those software licensors and software as a service (SaaS)/public cloud service providers who are able to insist on the use of their standard form contract terms will usually not budge on this point). However, while historically it might have been true to say that technology related contracts would always include such an exclusion, this is no longer the case. Some service providers have broken ranks and been willing to accept loss of profit as a claimable loss (at least insofar as it is a direct loss and subject to the overarching limits of liability) where the deal in question has been big/strategically important enough for them to feel that the additional risk was justified, which has in turn placed greater pressure upon those other service providers whose default position remains that they will not accept liability for such losses.

A potential compromise to consider may be to create a form of 'sub cap', ie, a smaller amount that sits within the overall liability cap (and forms part of it), and that can be claimed in relation to losses which are in the form of loss of profit/revenue. That way, the service provider mitigates its overall risk while the customer is comforted that while it still may not have full coverage for its potential exposure, the service provider at least has some 'skin in the game' so as to incentivise it to avoid the kinds of contract default that are likely to give rise to such losses.

For some service providers, such an approach may remain anathema on the basis that any reference to an acceptance of liability for loss of profit is visually/emotionally unacceptable, or may be seen as creating an unacceptable precedent. An alternative mechanism to consider in such circumstances, which avoids any overt mention of the concept of loss of profit or revenue, may be to create a form of 'super service credit' or liquidated damages payment which is linked to the kinds of defaults which would be most likely to give rise to a loss of profit. The upside for the service provider then is that it is able to maintain the position in good conscience that it has not expressly accepted liability for such losses, but with the downside that it then has an automatic exposure to the amount of the service credits/liquidated damages in question, regardless of whether or not the customer has in fact suffered such loss. The equivalent downside for the customer is that the amount of the service credits/liquidated damages are likely to be less than it would like (in recognition of the fact that it has an automatic right to be paid the relevant amounts, without being put to the trouble of actually proving its quantum of loss).

4.3 Loss of anticipated savings/benefits

A potential solution for the negotiating impasse in this regard may be to consider the nature of the anticipated savings/benefits themselves. If, for example, the anticipated saving is something that the service provider has in effect committed to achieve (eg, a reduction in cost for the in-scope services as against the amounts that the customer had previously been paying), then it may be possible to insert some 'for the avoidance of doubt' language to clarify that such amounts would still be claimable, should the customer need to bring the contract to an end and look elsewhere for the relevant services thereafter (as this would then in any event be in keeping with one of the core principles for a breach of contract related claim for damages, ie, so as to put the claimant in the position that they would have been in, had the contract been properly performed).

The next stage on from this may be to list out additional heads of savings which the parties can agree are not simply speculative and which should at least be claimable (albeit still on the basis that the customer would be put to the test of showing that the savings would in fact have been achieved, had the contract been performed, which may not be that easy in any event). A more customer friendly option may be to look at this from the opposite end of the spectrum, and to instead list out heads of anticipated savings that would not be claimable (on the basis that all other kinds of savings potentially would be claimable, at least to the extent that they could be argued to be a direct rather than an indirect head of loss).

4.4 Loss of goodwill/reputation

Compromise positions in relation to this head of loss are more difficult to come by, given the more significant uncertainties as to how such losses would be quantified or assessed. However, one particular option which we have seen employed in practice is to allow for a claim for costs of PR consultancies/brand consultants who may need to be engaged to help manage the fallout of a particular problem (eg, in the event of an IT security failure giving rise to unauthorised access to client data, it would likely be necessary to reach out to clients to assure them as to how the issue was being addressed, or possibly even conduct a form of media campaign to provide reassurance to the wider community). Another example we have seen was to specifically allow for the payment of a capped amount of *ex gratia* compensation to any end customers who might be impacted by a particular contract failure.

4.5 Loss or corruption of data

The identification of potential compromise positions in terms of this head of potentially excluded loss will depend in large part on the scope of the service provider's service obligations. Assuming that the supplier does not have express responsibility for making the customer's data backups, a potential compromise may be for the supplier to accept liability for the costs of recovering/reconstituting lost data arising as a result of its contract breach, but only back to the point when the last back up was, or ought to have been, made (ie, so that the service provider does not end up being responsible for losses that could have been avoided had the customer adopted a prudent/market standard data back up approach).

Another possibility may be to distinguish between liabilities associated between non-personal data (which may still be either claimable or which may remain excluded), and those which relate to personal data (which may again either be agreed to be claimable or excluded); see also the possibility of such losses being made subject to separate 'super caps, explained in Chapter 9.

4.6 Amounts payable to third parties

The customer may push back on such an exclusion from the outset, on the basis that if it can establish that it has had to incur such liabilities as a direct and natural consequence of the breach in question, then there is no good reason why it should not then be able to claim such losses (at least subject to the application of the overall cap on liability). The customer would argue in this regard that it would likely be already accepting the not-inconsiderable risk of many of such third-party claims being argued to be within the second limb of *Hadley v Baxendale* so as to be characterised as being an indirect loss and therefore likely to be excluded in any event.

If, however, the service provider maintains a tough line to this issue, potential compromise positions to consider include the following.

- Whether to include specific third parties or types of third-party claims within the list of deemed direct losses and so as to be confirmed as being expressly claimable in any event, and as an exception to the application of this head of exclusion. For example, it may be possible to specify that end client claims for compensation pursuant to a particular statutory scheme might be reimbursable, or that liabilities accruing to designated organisations or individuals may be claimable.
- Whether to allow for claims for such losses, but subject to a smaller sub cap within the scope of the wider liability cap (in a similar vein to the potential compromise approaches for claims for loss of profit, as discussed above).

13. Unlimited liabilities

1. Introduction

The treatment of unlimited liabilities is the third limb of the 'Holy Trinity' in terms of the liability provisions in technology contracts (the other two being the list of those types of losses which are excluded absolutely, and the setting of the monetary caps on whatever other heads of loss are claimable but on a limited basis).

Not surprisingly, the proposed heads of unlimited loss attract a lot of attention, as they are quite literally the potential 'bet the farm' provisions, ie, in the sense that in the worst case scenario, if a service provider were to be in default and cause catastrophic losses to the customer and such losses were then to fall into the unlimited bucket such that they could then be claimed back from the service provider, the service provider could potentially be put out of business as a result.

As is explained below, there are some of these types of loss which simply cannot be limited or excluded as a matter of law (and which as a result do not attract much negotiation attention in any event). There are others which tend to be seen as unlimited as a matter of market practice or convention. However, there are then other heads of loss which may be proposed to be recoverable on an unlimited basis which are less common, and which may therefore become much more contentious in the negotiation process.

2. The customer perspective

Clearly, the customer will start from the premise that it will want to reconfirm the position at law, *vis-à-vis* certain heads of loss which cannot be excluded or limited in any event (and indeed it is usually also in the service provider's interest that these also be set out. Under English law, for example, there would be a risk that the liability clause might otherwise be interpreted as purporting to exclude such losses, which might in turn give rise to a risk of the entire liability clause being ruled invalid).

The heads of loss which cannot be excluded or limited will vary depending on the governing law of the contract, but they will near universally include losses related to death or personal injury. Under English law, they will also include losses arising from fraud or fraudulent misrepresentation (as became a key focus for the famous UK technology dispute case of *BskyB v EDS* [2010] EWHC 86, where a successful assertion of fraudulent misrepresentation enabled the customer to sidestep a £30m limitation of liability and claim losses without limit, leading eventually to a settlement reported to be in excess of £300m), and also for losses arising from the warranties implied by law as to the ability to pass on good title, under the sale of goods and services legislation.

The customer will, however, also want to assert a right to claim other heads of loss on an unlimited basis (working on the assumption that it is unlikely to be able to get its preferred position overall, which would be to be able to claim for all its losses, without any limitation at all). The heads of loss it may therefore seek to recover on an unlimited basis are listed below.

2.1 Breach of intellectual property rights (IPR)

The customer's view in this regard is that it is trusting the service provider to have ensured that it has all of the requisite rights and consents to provide its products or services to the customer. It will argue that it has little, if any, ability to check or confirm that this is in fact the case, and as such it should be entirely at the risk of the service provider. The customer may also argue that it would be very difficult for it to quantify properly the potential exposure from IP-related claims, as it would not be able to predict who the potential litigant may be, what element of the service provider's products or deliverables the claim might relate to, or what the consequence might be (eg, ranging from a potential claim for compensation/a licence fee, through to being injuncted from making any use of the allegedly infringing materials).

The liabilities arising here will usually be linked to the wording of an IP indemnity clause, whereby the service provider also undertakes to indemnify and defend the customer against third-party IP infringement claims arising as a result of the service provider's services or products. The customer would ideally want such indemnity to cover all losses relating to such claims, ie, such that the unlimited liability element also covers its internal costs and losses, in addition to whatever amounts might ultimately need to be paid to the third-party claimant (either by way of a damages award or an agreed settlement).

2.2 Breach of confidentiality

A similar kind of argument will be run by the customer in respect of imposing unlimited liability for confidentiality breaches, ie, to the effect that it would be difficult if not impossible for it to predict the impact upon its business if the service provider were to breach its obligations of confidentiality. To take an extreme case, if the customer organisation was one which was itself heavily focused upon IP (say, for example, in relation to life sciences or pharma companies, or many technology companies), then unauthorised disclosures of information relating to its 'crown jewel' products might well cause irreparable harm to its business. Accordingly, the customer will want the service provider to maintain a laser-like focus upon preventing such confidentiality breaches, and having unlimited liability as a consequence is a powerful means of achieving this.

2.3 Data protection liabilities

As separately noted in Chapter 9, data protection liabilities are extremely topical and the drafting of contract terms in relation to them is in something of a state of flux. The customer will look at its increased risk profile – and in particular by reference to the possibility of genuinely massive General Data Protection Regulation (GDPR) related fines in the European Union and the associated risk of class action law suits – and argue that the only way that it can be adequately covered in respect of such risks is by way of unlimited liability.

2.4 Data and IT security obligations

Not all data is personal, of course, and the customer will also be extremely concerned as to the treatment of its commercial and business information. While there is an obvious overlap here with the obligations of confidentiality as set out above, the customer will also want to make sure that its data is not lost or corrupted, eg, by allowing malware to be introduced which might then irretrievably wipe valuable data or render it inaccessible. Again, the customer may seek to impose unlimited liability as a means of impressing upon the service provider just how crucial this is issue is to their business.

2.5 Official fines and sanctions

The customer may also seek to have any fines or monetary sanctions which may get imposed upon it by reason of the service provider's acts or omissions kept outside the limits of liability. Aside from again making the point that it would be very difficult for it to predict the quantum of any such awards, the customer may make the point that such amounts are not being paid to it, but will be instead be paid over (in effect) to the relevant regulator or official body. However, in more serious cases (which is where unlimited liability would be most likely to be of relevance in any event), the customer will likely also have suffered its own losses as a result of whatever gave rise to the official sanctions, and indeed will quite probably have accrued a termination right and so also be incurring the costs of having to swap service providers. If, then, its limit of liability *vis-à-vis* its potential recovery of such costs and losses has already been reduced (if not exhausted) by amounts which ultimately went into the coffers of the regulator etc, then the customer will be left without a meaningful remedy in respect of its own loss.

2.6 Wilful default/abandonment

The customer's argument in relation to wilful default (eg, where the service provider deliberately breaches the contract) or abandonment of it (eg, where the service provider ceases to perform the contract or a substantial part of it, without a *bona fide* belief that it has an entitlement to do so) is a relatively simple one. If the service provider has deliberately decided not to observe the terms of the contract, then it should equally not be entitled to avail itself of the protection of any of that contract's terms and conditions – including the limitations of liability. This also acts as a particular disincentive for a service provider to view the limit of liability as a form of 'termination fee' that it could pay/incur in return for getting out of the contract (which would be an extreme position, but one which has on occasion arisen in relation to the larger technology outsourcing agreements, if the service provider realises that it has fundamentally underestimated the cost of providing the services and so will be faced with making a substantial year-on-year loss in trying to perform it over the remainder of the term, while still facing a risk of claims and damages payments if it were to default at any point in trying to do so).

2.7 TUPE/Acquired Rights Directive

In relation to contracts where the contracts of existing employees may transfer by operation of law (ie, by way of the Transfer of Undertakings (Protection of Employment) Regulations 2006 (TUPE)), it is standard for the parties to agree that they will – on an unlimited and usually indemnified liability basis – accept liability for their own acts and omissions *vis-à-vis* the transferred employees, while such party was their employer (as such liabilities would other-wise transfer across to the new employer, along with the relevant employee). The argument in this regard is that the indemnifying party already has the relevant liability, whatever that may be, and as such the unlimited liability provision is simply making sure that the liability remains with the party who was responsible for it arising in the first place.

2.8   Breaches of law or regulation

In more recent times, more customers have pushed for a wider form of drafting regarding breaches of applicable law which go beyond the official fines and sanctions which may arise from them (as already mentioned above), and which instead impose unlimited liability for all consequences arising from breaches of law or regulation. The customer viewpoint in this regard is that such breaches may have more negative public relations/customer reputation impacts, and as such need to be avoided at all costs. Unlimited liability is therefore again used more as a 'stick' to impose greater focus upon compliance, rather than because the customer has a particular concern as to the quantum of its related financial losses.

2.9   Gross negligence

Unlimited liability is sometimes seen being imposed in respect of acts of 'gross' negligence. It should be said at the outset that such provisions are understandable in contracts which are subject to many civil law jurisdictions, where the concepts of liability and recoverable loss are focused more on degrees of culpability as opposed to remoteness (as is the case with the common law system). However, as many customers have businesses which operate in Europe as well as the United Kingdom, and so see contracts drafted pursuant to all manners of different governing laws, there has been a tendency for some to import the civil law concept of no limits applying for gross negligence, into contracts governed by English law.

The problem with this approach is that for many years the English courts did not recognise any difference between 'gross' negligence and 'normal' negligence, such that the effect of such a provision might well be to make any claims based on negligence (whether 'gross' or otherwise) sit outside the normal limits of liability (a position that would be to the customer's advantage in any event). Even if this position is challenged by the service provider, the customer may choose to get around the English law interpretation issue by simply giving gross negligence a defined meaning as a matter of contract drafting.

3.   The service provider perspective

Given the potential impact of an unlimited liability claim, it is not surprising that the service provider will approach the drafting of the unlimited liability provisions from exactly the opposite view-point as the customer, and will generally want to have as short a list of unlimited liabilities as is possible. As a side angle, if they are to accept unlimited liabilities, they will generally at least insist that such liabilities are expressed on a mutual basis (as many customer drafted contracts will be prepared such that the service provider's liabilities may be unlimited, but be silent about the customer's liability in the same or similar circumstances, which will ordinarily then have the effect of leaving any such potential claims subject to the main limit of liability provisions, whatever they may be set at).

3.1   Breach of IPR

The service provider may first seek to draw a distinction between its own products and services (where it is more likely to be willing to accept unlimited liability, on the basis that it will have a good sense of whether or not it has copied them from elsewhere) and those of a third party who just happen to form part of the overall solution. In the latter case, the service provider may argue that it has no ability to any substantive due diligence on that third party's products or services than the customer does, and that, accordingly the customer should simply get a 'flow through' of whatever IP-related liability protection the service provider itself is able to get from such third party.

In terms of its own products or services, the service provider will often seek to draw a distinction between claims regarding trademarks or copyright (on the basis that the service provider really should be able to assess and control such infringements) and claims relating to patents. In the latter case, because patents can be granted without the service provider having known about the competing claims/products, the service provider might argue that it should not then be faced with an unlimited liability claim in the event that it is subsequently found to have infringed a patent granted in favour of them.

If the unlimited liability provisions point back to the IP indemnity clause, the service provider will want to limit the unlimited liability exposure only to the amounts finally adjudged to be pay-able by way of damages to the third-party claimant (or by way of a settlement agreed to by the service provider), ie, and so as not to include the customer's own internal losses, which the service provider will say should fall within the liability cap in the same way as any other contractual loss claims would do.

3.2 Breach of confidentiality

While the service provider recognises the importance of keeping confidential material and information that is genuinely confidential, it will likely want to challenge the perspective that all information is in fact confidential, and moreover that it has a responsibility with regards to information the content of which it is aware. It would not be prudent, therefore, for it to accept unlimited damages with respect to an unknown and potentially unknowable risk. Additionally, with the rise of the GDPR legislation and the realistic potential for significant fines, a breach of the confidentiality provisions could be triggered in relation to the treatment of the personal data 'belonging' to the customer, such that the possible quantum of the potential loss it could incur would be intolerable: a genuine 'bet the company' position that no reasonable entity would accept.

3.3 Data protection liabilities

The service provider's perspective in relation to data protection liabilities will inevitably be one of heightened sensitivity, given the introduction of the significant fines under GDPR but also that the service provider itself could be directly fined by the relevant data protection authority if there was a breach of the data protection liability. Accepting a perceived 'double jeopardy' position of accepting significant liability to the customer in addition to that that might be imposed on it directly will, as indicated in Chapter 9, give rise to significant concerns.

3.4 Data and IT security obligations

In a similar vein to the confidentiality arguments outlined above, the service provider will likely be concerned as to the nature of the data that might give rise to the significant liability – the more sensitive the data is, the more significant the likely losses that the customer will be exposed to, and that it might seek to pass to the service provider. However, the service provider cannot model or understand the nature of this risk, as it does not know what is in the data – it 'sees' the customer's data only in its binary form (ie, a series of 1s and 0s), if at all. Not being able to quantify the risk means the service provider cannot accept a high level of liability, let alone unlimited.

Similarly, for the IT security obligations, the service provider will not think that these are (depending of course on the nature of the service) an absolute protection or guarantee on the part of the customer when it comes to IT security. The customer ought to be taking other measures to mitigate the risks of an IT security issue, which could happen irrespective of the service provider's acts and omissions. Accordingly, if the customer has these appropriate measures in place, the service provider should not need to accept unlimited liability.

3.5 Official fines and sanctions

The service provider's likely argument will be that it is not responsible for achieving the customer's compliance responsibilities; it is engaged to provide a service or a series of outputs. It remains for the customer to make sure that these are suitable to enable it to meet whatever laws and regulations the customer (and not the service provider) is obliged to meet. A customer cannot outsource regulatory compliance and therefore – the service provider will say – it cannot or should not pass on the financial consequences of that responsibility to the service provider.

Additionally, a service provider may be concerned that a regulatory authority, in imposing a fine, will look at issues beyond simply the service provider's acts or omissions, and that it is these other factors – such as past compliance issues, other relevant facts or the customer's approach to engagement with the regulatory over the relevant issues – that will result in a level of fine that is disconnected with the impact of the service provider's default. Accepting unlimited liability in such a situation would, therefore, expose the service provider to a level of liability that outweighs its own degree of responsibility.

3.6 Wilful default/abandonment

For a service provider, the concerns regarding any proposed imposition of unlimited liability in relation to these forms of default will likely centre on the actual definition of what is 'wilful' and 'abandonment'. If these are misconstrued or the interpretations go against it, then even if it had acted in a way that it believed was permitted under the agreement or if the act was committed by a rogue employee, the service provider would open itself to unlimited liability for a breach that otherwise would have been comfortably within the liability regime. This is a risk that many service providers will struggle to rationalise in such a way as to enable them to accept unlimited liability.

3.7 TUPE/Acquired Rights Directive

While a service provider might accept liability for its acts and omissions prior to any transfer of its own employees back to the customer or the customer's replacement service provider, it will probably want this to be mirrored in respect of any customer or third-party service provider staff that transfer to it on entry into the agreement. For some customers, this can be difficult if it has not obtained a 'back to back' indemnity from any incumbent service provider, and it will be too late at the relevant time for the customer to seek to obtain that coverage from its incumbent (and probably exiting) service provider.

Additionally, a service provider may be reluctant to agree an unlimited indemnity in respect of its employees that might transfer to the customer or a new service provider, on termination or expiry of the contract, so as to give the customer comfort that it will receive the services 'clean' on exit (eg, in terms of costs of making such staff redundant, as opposed to liabilities related to pre-transfer 'wrongdoing' in relation to their employment). The service provider's view in this respect will be driven for a variety of reasons, principal amongst which will be an unwillingness to put a competitor in a strong commercial position and the possibility of wanting, instead, a termination fee on exit, rather than having to incur unbudgeted and unpredictable costs when it is no longer earning revenue from the relevant account.

3.8 Breaches of law or regulation

Compliance with laws and regulations may be an important contractual obligation but it is simply another term of the agreement. It should not, therefore, attract a greater level of exposure than other breaches which would be accepted to be subject to the general cap on liability. Additionally, given the likely debates over which laws and regulations with which the service provider ought to be complying (in which respect, please see Chapter 3) a service provider will be reluctant to accept significant liability in respect of a body of laws and regulations that do not ordinarily apply to it.

3.9 Gross negligence

As recognised above, the distinction – under English law at least – between 'gross' negligence and 'normal' negligence is too fine a line to make sense of a justification of applying a liability cap to one side of the line, and unlimited liability to the other. If a definition of the term were to be agreed, to which unlimited liability were to apply, this would need to demonstrate a hugely significant disregard of the duty of care, and would therefore be more akin to a definition of wilful default. If liability for wilful default is already addressed, it would, therefore, be unnecessary to deal separately with liability for gross negligence.

3.10   Payment of the contract charges

The payment of contract charges is essential, and almost so obvious as to be not worthy of debate. If charges are payable, the customer's liability cap should not be used as a shield to defeat its payment obligations in respect of services that have been delivered and the customer has received and benefited from.

4.   Potential compromises

Finding a compromise on categories of unlimited liability (and of course liability provisions more generally) requires a clear understanding of both leverage and relevance. Understanding one's leverage or bargaining position is of course a fundamental part of any approach to negotiation, and to understanding the likely boundaries to which the discussions can be pushed in an effort to get the optimal solution. This is where relevance comes in. The relevance of requiring unlimited liability needs to be properly understood; whether it is relevant for the customer to require unlimited liability in a particular deal will of course depend on the particular circumstances and risks associated with that deal. In some transactions therefore it will be appropriate for the customer to expect unlimited liabilities and in others for the classification of unlimited liability to be much smaller. Clearly understanding the rationale behind each other's positions will result in a more appropriate allocation of risk.

With the foregoing in mind, the potential compromises below reflect a general allocation of risk and the state of market trends reflected in the unlimited liabilities provision at the time of writing.

One other key issue to bear in mind is the interplay between unlimited liability provisions and any exclusion of certain heads of loss. If these exclusions apply to the purportedly unlimited liability, the liability will not be unlimited in real terms. The parties' intention needs to be made clear in this respect.

4.1 Breach of IPR

It is relatively usual for the liability in respect of the IPR infringement indemnity to be unlimited, with the broader debate being had over the terms of the indemnity itself and the extent to which it covers any losses incurred by the customer in relation to the third-party claim, or simply the liability to the third party itself. Exceptions may be made in relation to patent liability, which may be limited to 'known' jurisdictions where the service provider could reasonably be asked to take on the infringement risk.

4.2 Breach of confidentiality

Notwithstanding the advent of GDPR-related liabilities, liability for breach of the confidentiality provisions again remains usually unlimited, albeit with a particular focus on what is covered by this unlimited liability. In this respect, it is increasingly common to see, as has been set out in this chapter, different treatments being applied to breach of confidence, data protection liability and data security liability, even though they can and frequently do result in the same issue – the unauthorised disclosure of confidential material to a third party.

Consequently, the liability regimes relating to agreements which will result in the service provider processing personal data or having the possibility of affecting access to it, will separate breaches of the confidentiality provisions relating to personal data from the unlimited liability for confidential information, so that they can be dealt with via a separate regime.

4.3 Data protection liabilities

As a consequence of the rise of the GDPR, data liability is now often treated separately. Very often this is now subject to its own cap on liability, separate from the general cap, and some magnitude higher than the general cap (ie, a 'super cap'). When structuring this cap, it is important to consider what ought to be included inside the cap and what should not. In respect of a breach of data protection provisions, for example, the likely losses might include: fines from a data protection authority, remedial steps to resolve the breach, claims from affected third parties, remedial activities for affected data subjects (eg, credit monitoring), internal investigation costs and so forth. If all of this is to be subject to the data protection liability cap, this needs to be taken into account so that the cap is sufficient.

There might also be some data protection related liability that ought not to be subject to the cap, such as 'wrong pocket' liability arising as a consequence of the application of Article 82 of GDPR.

Finally, if data protection liability is to be capped, then it would be worth considering the interplay between the data protection cap and the general cap so as, from a customer benefit, to obtain the 'highest' level of protection possible, for example, by adding the general cap to the data protection cap in certain circumstances.

4.4   Data and IT security obligations

Because the impact of a breach of the data and IT security provisions is often felt in the confidentiality and the data protection provisions (ie, a disclosure of confidential material or personal data), it is not uncommon for this liability for a breach of these provisions to track the positions on those two sets of terms. Of course, in some larger scale outsourcing transactions, where one of the service provider's core responsibilities is to maintain the security of an IT infrastructure, a more bespoke approach may well be more appropriate, especially where the service provider is responsible for determining the level of security to be applied to systems and solutions.

4.5   Official fines and sanctions

Whist there can be some debate as to the possibility of requiring a service provider to be liable for fines imposed on a customer (on the basis that it is potentially not possible, in broad terms, to require a third party to underwrite exposure to fines), fines imposed on a customer as a consequence of the service provider's breach of the agreement and characterised therefore as damages flowing from a breach of contract, and not some form of insurance policy, are often set out on an unlimited basis. This is especially the case in outsourcing agreements in regulated sectors and particularly where the service provider's services are business process services such that – while the service provider is not responsible for the customer's regulatory compliance – its contribution to achieving it is so fundamental it ought to take a larger portion of responsibility for it.

If this is agreed, then often there will be mechanisms to adjust the service provider's liability in the event that the quantum of the fine is not directly associated with their breach, eg, is higher because of the customer's past compliance performance or because the regulatory authority took into account other breaches as well.

The parties need to consider carefully the interaction between this liability and that relating to data protection.

4.6 Wilful default/abandonment

The key to unlocking any debate on this provision is to be clear over the definitions of the terms 'wilful default' and 'abandonment'. If the parties can agree on definitions that point to a deliberate or very reckless actions, that point to a behaviour that disregards the terms of the agreement (and therefore would indicate that the liability cap should not apply), this will often be agreed to be unlimited. A potential compromise alternatively may be to agree a separate cap which is sufficiently large to act as a meaningful disincentive for the service provider to ever decide to simply 'walk away' from the project in question.

4.7 TUPE/Acquired Rights Directive

The position achieved in relation to the TUPE/Acquired Rights Directive will depend on the broader commercial arrangements between the parties, especially insofar as it is the service provider's solution and whether, for example, it is employing staff specifically for the performance of the services to the customer, whether it inherited staff on entrance into the agreement and the existence and extent of any termination fee.

Additionally, the TUPE/Acquired Rights Directive position on entry will influence the position on exit. Many parties will agree to a 'clean on entry, clean on exit' position in relation to TUPE, meaning that each will indemnify each other on an unlimited basis with respect to employment liabilities and the costs associated with transferring employees on entry, in the case of the customer, and on exit, in the case of the service provider.

4.8 Breaches of law or regulation

Often, this will be dealt with under the heading of the official fines and sanctions, discussed above, which might cover not just the fine but also the costs of carrying out any activities to remediate the failures that gave rise to the fine.

Beyond this, whether this liability should be unlimited will depend on the size of the general cap and the nature of the services, particularly with respect to the extent that the services are of a regulated nature. In forming a position on this issue, the parties will need to reflect on the negotiated position on compliance with laws and in particular, which laws the service provider is in fact responsible for complying with, as discussed in Chapter 3.

4.9 Gross negligence

In some legal systems and in respect of some contracts, unlimited liability in respect of gross negligence is relatively market standard. In more 'traditional' sourcing and technology contracts governed by English law, it is less common. If the parties have a serious breach of duty in mind that would constitute 'gross' negligence, then they would do well to define this in the agreement, and in doing so, consider its interplay with any definition of 'wilful default' or 'abandonment'.

4.10 Payment of the contract charges

Commonly, liability for properly due and undisputed charges would sit outside of the liability cap, but a customer will want to be clear that the charges to which this relates are those that it is actually obliged to pay under the terms of the agreement in respect of the services and not some broader classification of charges that might include additional amounts payable to the service provider as a consequence of the customer's defaults that has resulted in the service provider having to carry out more work, which would perhaps be better determined to be damages resulting from a breach of contract.

In summary, determining the unlimited liabilities is of course a function of risk allocation as between the parties revolving around considerations of fault, leverage, relevance, oversight, likelihood and an assessment (or perception) of which party is better placed to bear the risk. With this in mind, a careful assessment of the reality of the arrangements being put in place and the respective commercial 'realpolitik' will likely drive the outcomes in respect of the unlimited liability discussions. In this respect, it is of course worth noting that negotiations concerning unlimited liabilities are not, or should not be, 'all or nothing' conversations. That is, if a party will not agree to accept unlimited liability, the only resultant answer is not that it is therefore capped at the general cap or is not covered. With some thought and flexibility, it is possible to agree a more sophisticated liability résumé that allocates liability for certain heads of loss between the parties in a more precise and specific way, perhaps via a series of caps that achieves for both parties a sensible and fair allocation of risk and liability.

14. TUPE in outsourcing agreements

1. Introduction

1.1 Overview of TUPE regulations

As organisations seek to improve their processes, move from one provider to another to effect change or to digitally transform to remain competitive it is likely that the human aspects will become more of a factor. Specifically, in a large sourcing arrangement there is often likely to be a team from the service provider providing the service to the customer on a dedicated, or partially dedicated, basis. Alternatively, where a customer is contemplating an outsource for the first time, there is likely to be a customer group of employees who currently perform some or all of the activities which are in scope for the service provider to take over.

As such, the potential for the application of the Transfer of Undertakings (Protection of Employment) Regulations 2006 (TUPE) (reflecting the Acquired Rights Directive in the EU) arises and so it is essential to understand:

- the regulations themselves;
- when TUPE applies;
- who and what actually transfers under the regulations;
- what constitutes fair or unfair dismissal in connection with such a process;
- the requirements for consultation and information provision;
- who is liable for pre- and post-transfer redundancy; and
- how these issues play out in commercial negotiations.

1.2 How TUPE applies

In summary, TUPE exists to protects employees so that when their work is outsourced/sourced from a third party, their employment follows. While TUPE is a UK statute, it derives from European legislation (the Acquired Rights Directive, as discussed further below) and so similar considerations apply to sourcing arrangements across Europe.

Where the legislation does apply, and the employees are protected, it means the following.

- *For a first time outsource.* This means that those customer employees who are mainly active in the transferring activities automatically become the service provider's employees upon the outsource.
- *For a reprocurement.* This means that those incumbent employees who are mainly active in the transferring activities automatically become new employees of the service provider upon the outsource (or employees of the customer (if there is an insource).

The effect of TUPE is that those transferring employees will transfer to the (new) supplier or back to the customer as the case may be, on the same terms and conditions as they had previously enjoyed with the customer or the incumbent supplier.

A key factor to remember is that it is not possible to contract-out of the legislation. As a result, as part of the preparations for a sourcing arrangement, the customer and service provider are required by law to follow a prescribed information and consultation process with the affected employees. As part of the overall commercial negotiation, however, the customer and service provider will also negotiate, and allocate, between them, the various potential risks/liabilities which are associated with those transferring employees. Although consideration of these country-specific details lies beyond the scope of this book, it is important to note, therefore, that additional country-specific requirements and issues may therefore arise should a project involve potential transfers of staff across multiple European countries.

Outside of the EU, there are some similar (but not identical) legal regimes, but the most common position, is that there will be no automatic transfer of customer's employees (or those of its incumbent suppliers). The parties will, therefore, need to reflect in their contract any additional obligations that they may want to apply (eg, any obligation upon the service provider to make offers of employment to the customer's in-scope personnel).

1.3 The European legal backdrop

The European legislation by which, in certain circumstances, customer employees automatically follow the outsource is the European Acquired Rights Directive (ARD). Each European member state has its own legislation implementing the ARD into its domestic law.

1.4 When TUPE applies

The typical legal analysis of any potential employee transfer in the EU can be reduced to four steps.

- *Step 1*. Does the legislation apply?
- *Step 2*. Who transfers?
- *Step 3*. What transfers?
- *Step 4*. What are the information and consultation requirements?

1.5 Step 1: Does the legislation apply?

Broadly, the legislation applies when there is a 'relevant transfer'. In the United Kingdom, TUPE goes wider than the ADR and two tests determine whether or not particular circumstances give rise to a relevant transfer: the 'business transfer test' and the 'service provision change test'.

What are we testing? It must be remembered that the purpose of this analysis is to assess whether a group of employees (or even an individual) will be 'caught' (protected) by the TUPE legislation as part of a sourcing or outsourcing deal. If so, then the employee(s) are what is termed a 'relevant transfer'; meaning that the law will operate to move the jobs of those affected employees from one party to another (from the customer to the service provider, from the service provider to a new supplier, or even from the service provider back to the customer on an insource).

(a) The tests themselves

This is about the identity of the transferring group. If the group of employees retains its 'identity' following the change of supplier then the test is satisfied. If the test is satisfied that means that TUPE will apply; and the terms and conditions of employment of those people will be preserved.

As per TUPE, the group needs to be "an organised grouping of employees situated in Great Britain which has as its principal purpose the carrying out of the activities concerned on behalf of the customer". 'Principal purpose' means that the employees must be essentially dedicated to the relevant activity. Further, it must be that the parties intend that following the change of provider, the service provider will carry out essentially the same activities.

So, in the United Kingdom, TUPE will apply if one or both of these tests are satisfied. The tests are not clear-cut, and application varies across Europe. As such, it is common for the terms and conditions of a sourcing agreement to detail the implications of TUPE's application just in case TUPE is triggered.

1.6 Step 2: Who transfers?

The question of who transfers comes down to the extent to which an employee is 'assigned' to the part of the business which is transferring. If they are, then they are taken to automatically transfer. This means that on the date of the actual transfer the employment contracts of those staff are deemed to have been made between the employee and the service provider (or new supplier, or customer on an insource etc). So the terms are preserved, including continuity of employment. For example, an individual working on a particular project could end up with 10 years continuity, having worked for three years at the customer, then six years at supplier #1 and then a year at supplier #2.

As such, while 'who transfers' because they are 'assigned' to a part of the business is a matter of fact, there will typically be discussion between customer and the service provider as to the way the services under the agreement are performed. For example, a customer will often seek contractual terms to require a service provider to organise its service delivery in such a way so that the risk of a transfer on exit is minimised.

1.7 Step 3: What transfers?

The general rule is that all rights and liabilities relating to a transferring employee transfer with them. Of course, there will be exceptions to this general rule. As such, while claims for non-payment of wages will 'stick to' the relevant employee and transfer with him or her, rights relating to old age or ill-health retirement under occupational schemes may not.

This means that as part of negotiation, the parties will seek to agree the allocation of liabilities and ultimately the costs of those liabilities. So, while the sourcing agreement cannot prevent a transfer, it can deal with who pays, and might require a customer to reimburse a service provider (for example) where those costs had been caused by the customer before the transfer date. This is the market standard position and is rarely – if ever – resisted during the course of the negotiation of the TUPE-related provisions.

1.8 Step 4: What are the information and consultation requirements?

TUPE requires the provision of relevant information concerning the transferring employees. The list is set out in the legislation and includes, as you might expect, sufficient information to identify the type of employee (but without giving personal details such as name and address). More importantly for the assessment of the likely costs of taking on the group of staff, information must be provided as to the pay and other terms and conditions of employment. Another key aspect which goes to the assessment of potential liability is that information must be given regarding recent disciplinary action.

Not only must prescribed information be given, but it must be provided in a timely way; specifically at least 28 days before the transfer (although of course in reality, the sourcing contract is likely to seek to vary that period, often as part of exit assistance provisions, so that the information is provided much earlier so as to allow for better planning).

In addition to information provision requirements, the current employer has a duty to consult with the relevant employees. That consultation will include providing information about the deal and about the impact of the transfer. The point of consultation is to seek to reach agreement with the affected employees regarding any new measures which might be planned. Such measures could include dismissals, or changes to terms and conditions. Consultation is a crucial part of the process, and a decision to award a sourcing or outsourcing contract should not be made until the consultation has been concluded. Further, failure to consult carries potential financial consequences for the customer and supplier in the form of up to 13 weeks' pay per affected employee.

2. The customer perspective

From the customer's perspective, a typical key part of the business case for a first-time outsource in particular is the cost savings that can be achieved by removing, in whole or part, a (costly) part of the customer's business, changing instead to paying a service charge for a (better?) service from the service provider. What that means in plain terms is that it is likely that customer staff will be affected. That brings with it a mixture of implications.

- The customer will no longer need to employ a non-core function, saving money (particularly if that function was previously provided from a costly location). For example, should a 'back-office' function for a bank, such as printing or IT support, be provided from costly City premises, or can it be provided remotely, perhaps from an off-shore location such as Eastern Europe or India? However, loss of that function could risk loss of 'corporate memory', albeit for non-core elements of the organisation.

The customer will accordingly need to ensure that key staff are retained by the service provider if possible (or at least for an agreed period of time), and find a way to be happy that some of its previous staff will transfer, presumably continue their role, and provide the customer with the same services; save that (of course) the customer wants one of the outcomes of the outsourcing to be an improvement in the service it receives. One key question is: how can these two intensions be reconciled?

• In a secondary outsource (from incumbent to new provider) the customer will wish to step-back from any TUPE implications so far as is possible, and (contractually) create a situation where the liabilities for transferring staff are a matter for the two suppliers themselves, and not a concern for the customer.

For a first-time outsource, the customer will accordingly need to be proactive, and carry out due diligence on its current workforce so as to assemble the required information in a timely way, and to ascertain the extent of the likely transferring employees.

2.1 Can TUPE be avoided?

Customers sometimes seek to avoid TUPE altogether; the rationale being that taking-on existing staff will be costly for the service provider – a cost which will be charged back to the customer as part of the service charge. It might also be that the service provider wishes to avoid the application of TUPE altogether – it may not want to take on staff and would much rather prefer to provide the required service from its existing team.

As set out earlier, the business transfer test and service provision change test will be critical in making this assessment. A helpful summary of the case law and issues to consider when assessing the business transfer test can be found in the case of *Cheesman v R Brewer Contracts Ltd* [2001] IRLR 144 but an increasingly key aspect is known as the 'fragmentation' assessment. This is relevant because most larger deals involve a transformation element. It is becoming less and less the case that outsourcing is merely a transfer of an 'as-is' service ('your mess for less') and instead a customer will wish to leverage the expertise of the service provider to gain competitive advantage, transforming technology, outputs and business processes.

That means that it can sometimes be argued that the services to be provided by the incoming service provider are sufficiently different such that the grouping of staff (the undertaking) no longer retains its identity.

A change in contractual outcome can be useful evidence of fragmentation. If a customer moves from a sole-source to a best-of-breed multi-source arrangement then there will be a change from a single contract to many commercial arrangements running in parallel, and then it might be that TUPE does not apply (ie, on the basis that there is no longer a single defined 'undertaking' that the employees can be associated with, as opposed to several).

2.2 Is it desirable that TUPE is applied?

A customer might actually want TUPE to apply to ensure continuity of service. Those same staff who it used to employ know the organisation, and can help the service provider to ensure that their solution works with the processes and politics of the customer organisation.

That said, a customer may equally want to improve the way it receives a service, either because it no longer feels that the home-team are providing a modern service, or because the incumbent provider's service has become tired. As such, the customer will want to avoid a full TUPE transfer, because it risks receiving the same service from the same staff now employed by the service provider.

The customer may need to require the service provider to continue to provide the service from the same jurisdiction, or from a location near to the customer's own. This is often the case where speed of reaction time is a factor, or where the nature of the services themselves are particularly sensitive, perhaps involving the processing of confidential data of some kind. Alternatively, where those factors are not present, the customer may well be looking for an off-shore solution to take advantage of huge differences of input-cost and thereby save money.

As such the customer will want to drive behaviours by the terms and conditions that it proposes, particularly in the request for proposal (RfP) documentation in a competitive outsource bid process. Of course, if a customer is seeking to enjoy savings offered by offshoring, there may be upfront redundancy costs to be paid. The same is true of a move from traditional on-premise technology service provision to a cloud solution. A typical cloud hosting solution will be offered 'at a distance'; most likely from a different jurisdiction. Again, redundancy costs will become a factor if staff roles disappear.

While a customer with strong contractual leverage will seek to pass those costs to the service provider, the reality is that the customer will end up paying, one way or another; either directly through the redundancies themselves, or indirectly in the charge-back from the service provider as part of the agreement charges.

3. The service provider perspective

From a service provider's perspective, the initial requirement is information, and lots of it. The service provider will need sufficient detail of the nature of the activities undertaken by the staff, the services they provide, and all of their employment contract details so that it can factor those into its own approvals process and business case development. Indeed, where a service provider is participating in a competitive outsourcing process, it will need this detail to be comprehensive so that it can propose a price without the need for huge amounts of caveats.

There is a subtle difference in service provider perspective, dependent upon whether that supplier is a new supplier (perhaps in a first time outsource) and whether it is the incumbent supplier for a project which is being competitively re-tendered. This is further explained below.

3.1 New supplier view

As a potential new supplier for a customer requirement, the service provider will be considering whether the relevant staff are useful, and might help to provide the services required. The key question is: why would a service provider want such staff? Clearly, they will have detailed inside information as to the culture of the customer's organisation, the centres of power and influence, as well as any inherent inefficiencies which might not be apparent from an RfP. They will also be familiar/skilled in relation to the underlying services.

The flip-side is also true: a service provider with a key skill, offering, or reputation might want to ensure that only its own staff are involved in the provision of the services. That way it can ensure that its own staff are aligned with the service provider culture, approach, methodologies and so forth, thereby ensuring that the service provider can deliver the service it is offering and not be hindered by ex-customer staff.

A key factor will be whether the customer in the procurement documentation has actually specified whether TUPE does or does not apply. Often, in an RfP the customer will have stated that TUPE will apply. The service provider need not take this at face value and, provided that it is able to perform sufficient due diligence, it may be able to take a different view. Then as part of its RfP submission, the service provider can use this analysis as an attractive argument to support a lower price.

Whatever the approach, and however the service provider wishes to frame its response, the message is clear: staff issues need early attention in the bid process which means active due diligence and engagement with the customer.

3.2   The incumbent supplier's view

In terms of an incumbent supplier, similar considerations apply to those described above, but the perspective is different: from the incumbent's viewpoint it will be important to take a view as to which staff are essential to retain. The service provider who is in the incumbent supplier position will be facing the real possibility of losing the customer's business. As such, while it is seeking to win the reprocurement it is being forced to assist the customer and other bidders with their due diligence, against its commercial better interests.

The incumbent's viewpoint is further complicated if it becomes likely that the incumbent will not be re-awarded the contract. In that situation the incumbent's viewpoint flips: the service provider would face the loss of a key contract, and the overhead of a cohort of staff who have nothing to do. Of course, some of those staff can be absorbed into the service provider organisation or redeployed on other matters, but there may be a rump of staff who will need to be made redundant. In this instance the service provider will be keen to ensure that TUPE does apply so that it can avoid redundancy costs, or else seek to negotiate commercial terms to pass some or all of the costs of such redundancies on to the customer (particularly if some or all of such staff were transferred from the customer and/or its legacy suppliers at the commencement of the contract with the service provider).

3.3   Cherry picking and lemon dropping

'Cherry picking' and 'lemon dropping' are now common phrases used to describe the assessment of the existing workforce, and how they might be structured. As such the 'cherries' (the really valuable staff) might be reassigned before the transfer in such a way as to fall outside of the ambit of the transferring undertaking, whereas the 'lemons' (the less valuable staff, or ones with known employment issues such as absenteeism, etc) might be pushed more evidently into the undertaking so that the current employer can legitimately (and probably gratefully) lose them to the transferee.

The extent to which a service provider is able to do this, or a customer is able to regulate this behaviour, will depend on the terms of the relevant agreement, and it is common to feature express wording to deal with restructuring of this sort, eg, by restricting any changes to the makeup of the team of people engaged within the relevant function once a termination notice has been served, or within a set period to its expiry.

4.   Potential solutions

4.1   Disagreement as to TUPE application

As described earlier, one of the first questions to ask in any sourcing or outsourcing situation is whether or not TUPE will apply. In many kinds of delivery-orientated IT contract, it won't be relevant as there is no 'undertaking' being transferred (eg, in the case of a software licence arrangement, or one-off software delivery project). However, from the commercial perspective, both parties should consider whether they actually want TUPE to apply, even if there is such an undertaking to be transferred. The answer to this question will depend on the commercial objectives and perspective of each party.

Disagreement as to whether TUPE applies to the facts at hand, and the staff forming part of the undertaking is a vexed situation which can delay the conclusion of the contract. Indeed, we have seen such issues left far too late in the process, time and again, and seen the commercial negotiations finalise and be replaced with detailed employment law negotiations (with the risk that employment specialists are brought in too late, and are not aware of the wider commercial context).

The disagreement needs to be resolved. The alternative is a costly remediation. If, for example, a team of staff successfully claim that they should have transferred, but the incoming service provider refuses to employ them, then the staff will likely claim against both the customer and service provider for redundancy pay, unfair dismissal, notice pay and for a failure to consult.

4.2   First time outsource

In a first time outsource, part of the rationale for the outsource itself is likely to be cost-savings and so the customer will often wish to ensure that TUPE does apply, and that the entire cohort of relevant staff are transferred to the incoming service provider (and so get them off its payroll, and preferably without redundancy costs).

This will be acceptable, subject to terms, so long as the service provider has comprehensive detail of the relevant staff at an early enough stage to enable it to assess the likely costs, and so that it can investigate how those transferring staff can assist with service provision.

The exact number of staff to transfer should be examined in detail and a consensus reached. Through this process it may become apparent that the actual number to transfer are less than originally anticipated by the customer. That may be advantageous to both parties: the customer will retain an 'intelligent customer function' staffed by employees who understand the legacy service and who can assist with transition to the new service provider's solution. Equally, the service provider's bid may be more attractive in financial terms if the customer can reassign some staff so as to avoid the need for them to be made redundant.

If, however, the service provider doesn't itself need the customer's in-scope personnel (perhaps because it wants to move the services offshore, or replace human labour with automated/ software driven solutions), the parties will need to negotiate a purely commercial solution. This will usually involve either the customer itself making the staff redundant, via appropriate compromise agreements with them prior to the contract taking effect, or the service provider being reimbursed or indemnified by the customer for the costs of any post-transfer redundancies. This also opens up the possibility of more imaginative 'gainshare' style arrangements, whereby the service provider may be financially incentivised to retrain or redeploy some of the customer's transferring staff, by allowing the service provider to retain a proportion of what would otherwise have had to have been paid to them by way of redundancy, if it can in fact find continuing roles for them within its business.

4.3 First time offshore

Moving the services out of the jurisdiction, or to a new technology such as a cloud hosting service, will inevitably mean redundancies. That will be unsettling for the rest of the customer's employees and so careful handling of the communications is essential. Equally, the customer will need to assess whether the staff can be absorbed and reassigned to minimise this disruption, while not destroying the business case for the offshoring.

4.4 Incumbent to new supplier transfer

As said above, a key concern for the customer where there is a change of supplier is to structure the agreement terms so far as is possible so that the TUPE issues are for the two suppliers to resolve, with minimal involvement of the customer. The exit assistance provisions will be key in this regard.

4.5 What if there is more than one new supplier?

Where a service is moved to a multi-source arrangement the issue becomes complicated; specifically, as to which staff are assigned to which elements of the service (and so should transfer to which supplier).

The parties concerned can resolve this through negotiation and a pragmatic approach will be to spread the relevant employees across the relevant contracts; thereby sharing the financial liability, and at the same time protecting the relevant staff across the landscape of new contracts.

4.6 Information

As stated earlier, the TUPE process, and the angst caused in negotiations, is a direct factor of the adequacy, accuracy and completeness of the employee data. If the data is correct, the incoming service provider can be definitive in its pricing, if it is incorrect then the service provider must price on the basis of assumptions and dependencies. It is not uncommon for staff data to be unavailable at the time of contract conclusion and so this becomes a prime candidate for post-contract variation.

Even with the best data available, it is common for contract clauses to deal (by way of indemnity) for unexpected redundancy costs (eg, the staff who were not known about/disclosed, but who can then successfully assert a right to transfer to the service provider). The extent of the indemnity will be negotiated and it needs to be clear as to whether the indemnity is merely for the unexpected redundancy cost, or whether it goes further and also encompasses 'employee liabilities'. This is the approach taken in standard public sector contracts. The 'employee liabilities' will go further than mere redundancy, and include liabilities arising due to the employment itself, such as disciplinary actions and discrimination claims, unfair dismissal liabilities. It will also set out whether 'redundancy' means merely statutory redundancy pay, or also include (usually more substantial) contractual entitlements, discretionary redundancy packages, payments to compensate for missing notice and pension entitlements that may be triggered by redundancy (known collectively as Beckmann liabilities).

4.7 How is this captured contractually?

This is captured in the following ways.

- *Indemnity*. Usually the customer will indemnify the service provider for employment liabilities (subject to an acceptable definition of what those liabilities actually are but typically including any claims of harassment, discrimination, arrears in pay etc, so as to effectively cover all employment-related 'wrong-doing' that pre-dated the transfer) that transfer to the service provider along with the staff themselves.
- *Information*. A customer will also usually agree to stand behind the accuracy of the data it shares.
- *Service provider indemnity*. While the customer will likely indemnify for issues that pertain to the period prior to the transfer, the service provider will usually indemnify the customer for issues arising due to the service provider's acts or omissions while it is the employer of the staff, post transfer.
- *Supplier to supplier protection*. As above, it is usual for the incoming new supplier to gain protection from the outgoing incumbent. Whether this is given by the outgoing service provider themselves, or sought from the ultimate customer, will be a matter for negotiation.
- *TUPE process indemnities*. It is usual for cross-indemnity protection to be agreed between the parties as to the required TUPE process activities. These will include the consultation process itself and whether it has been undertaken in accordance with the regulations.
- *Indemnity scope*. The parties will need to agree whether the indemnities agreed above are for awarded sums (only) or go further and capture the costs of claims, process, external advice and so forth. It will be a matter for relative leverage to decide whether the indemnities are narrow or wide in this way, acknowledging that TUPE disputes can be messy, complex and therefore expensive.
- *Exit provisions interplay*. The contract should also deal with the information provision requirements, assistance requirements and the risks associated with cherry picking and lemon dropping (as discussed previously). As such it is normal to address the extent to which the relevant staff can be reallocated (or not), what information should be collected and retained

during the term of the agreement, and what information can be made available for a termination, partial termination, agreement expiry or decision to insource. An element which is often missed is that information can be called upon by the customer. Typically, a standard exit schedule will only allow that information drop to be made once, a few months prior to expiry or termination. However, increasingly customers are seeking to reorganise their service provision, perhaps taking elements of the bundled service away from the incumbent, leaving that agreement in place but entering into additional contracts for parts of the legacy service. To do so, the customer will need detailed information with which to write the relevant RfP and to negotiate and conclude the agreement with the new supplier. This means that there is a need for an express right to call for that information during the term.

In summary, the message is clear as regards the TUPE elements of a technology project: TUPE shouldn't be treated as a stand-alone activity. Rather, it is indelibly linked to the commercial profile of the overall deal, carrying with it serious commercial considerations for both parties. As such, information about the service scope and the staff currently involved in that scope will need to be available, and considered in great detail so as to ensure that the right balance of risk and reward is struck.

A working knowledge of TUPE law, redundancy, pensions and so forth is also essential, but it is likely that specialist colleagues will need to form part of the team. Organising this shouldn't be left too late in the process. There are examples of deals which have derailed through last minute attention to staff issues.

Lastly, the human elements should not be forgotten; a change of employer is unsettling for those concerned and also those left behind. Carried out correctly, this can be seen as a new chapter: career progression with a true win-win for the service provider, the customer and the affected staff.

15. Termination rights

1. Introduction

In the ideal world, a project will run without a hitch until its natural conclusion (be that in terms of the completion of defined services and/or delivery of identified work products, or the completion of a pre-set time period). However, in practice things do not always run to plan, and accordingly a contract will often need to consider what kind of circumstances may justify either party being able to call a halt to the engagement.

It is important to note that, under English law, it will be possible to terminate a contract even in the absence of any express contract provisions to entitle a party to do so (at least in the absence of express additional contract drafting to preclude such rights, as we will return to in more detail, below). However, the threshold for termination is then very high. One would have to show that the other party has committed a 'repudiatory breach' (which, without delving too much into black letter law, would be a breach of a provision which has been expressly identified as a condition of the contract, or a breach of some other provision of the contract which is severe/material enough to deprive the non-breaching party of substantially all of the intended benefit of the contract). It is far more common, therefore, for the parties to pre-identify certain specific circumstances where a termination of the relevant contract would be permissible, albeit that the scope and triggers for such termination will vary significantly from contract to contract, and depending on the nature of the services involved. It is equally important to note that – again unless the contract specifically provides to the contrary – these termination rights would then apply in addition to the common law repudiatory breach termination right, rather than in place of it.

This chapter, accordingly, considers some of the typical termination provisions that one might expect to see in a technology contract, and particularly those for longer-term/ongoing services (such as managed service or outsourcing agreements).

2.   The customer perspective

It is obviously in the customer's interests to have as broad a scope of termination rights as is possible. Aside from the options that it may then have available to it in the event that things go wrong in future or in the event that the project otherwise fails to meet its commercial expectations, the existence of a potential termination right will be a powerful lever for the customer to have available to it to assist in any potential renegotiations that it may then have with its service provider. That said, customers should be well advised not to push too hard in this regard. If a service provider believes that it is exposed to 'hair trigger' termination rights, it will feel less secure in making investments in the services and the wider relationship, and may load additional risk premium into its pricing. Fear of a constant 'Sword of Damocles' hanging over its head in the form of a potential contract termination may also impact upon its day to day behaviours (eg, working to the letter of the contract rather than in an open and collaborative manner).

With that context, typical termination rights which customers may seek can be summarised in the categories that follow below.

2.1   Insolvency

If the service provider is insolvent, it will either be unable to provide the required services in any event (eg, if it has actually gone into liquidation or has otherwise ceased day to day operations) or will be facing a significant likelihood of disruption in trying to do so (eg, if the service provider has gone into administration and so is technically still in operation, but is then facing difficulties in terms of gaining further supplies from its own supply chain and subcontractors, and potentially in retaining its key personnel engaged in the services). The customer will, therefore, typically push for an express termination trigger linked to a set of defined circumstances which would suggest that the service provider either is already insolvent or will likely become so, for example:

- the service provider is unable to pay its debts when due;
- the service provider is subject to an order or a resolution for its liquidation, administration, winding up or dissolution (at least unless this is part of a *bona fide* solvent corporate amalgamation or reconstruction);
- the service provider has an administrative or other receiver, manager, trustee, liquidator, administrator or similar office appointed over all or a substantial part of its assets;

- the service provider enters into a composition or arrangement with its creditors; or
- the service provider suffers any analogous event or proceeding in any applicable jurisdiction.

Note that there is an argument from the customer perspective that waiting until the service provider has become insolvent is actually too late, as by then the customer may be faced with a disorganised scramble to repatriate its services and data in circumstances where the service provider may not be in a position to assist and/or may also be distracted by the demands of multiple other clients. On that basis, the customer may push for an anticipatory termination right, which would be exercisable at some point before the service provider is actually insolvent, but so as to give the customer more opportunity to exit from the service provider services in an orderly way and with assistance from the service provider and its personnel. As can be anticipated, such provisions can be hotly debated (as the service provider supplier may seek to argue that it is suffering a short-term financial squeeze from which it can recover and so should not then face the loss of its contract. Indeed, it may argue that its ability to avoid insolvency might be adversely impacted in the event that the customer – and potentially other clients – have the right to pull their contracts and the associated revenues associated with them. The customer can seek to address these concerns by either providing that there must be some degree of reasonableness requirement to its assessment that the service provider is likely to suffer any of the insolvency events referred to above or if the service provider is still unhappy as to the residual level of subjectivity that this still involves, linking the termination right to some other factual/ objective event, such as a breach of a banking covenant or if the service provider's credit rating with someone like Moody's or Standard & Poor's drops to or below a set level.

2.2 Material breach

Perhaps the most common termination trigger is the one linked to breach of contract. Typically, this is related to a 'material' breach of contract (ie, so as not to allow the contract to be terminated for minor, inconsequential breaches, although ironically the English Courts have ruled in the case of *Great Yarmouth v Rice* that a termination clause allowing termination for any breach of contract should in fact be interpreted as then requiring any such breach to be repudiatory in nature, and so it is clear that some very precise drafting is required in this regard). If this is the case, the customer will need to be specific as to whether the termination trigger is to be a material breach of any term of the contract, or any breach of a material term. The circumstances of termination would be potentially very different, depending on which formulation is chosen.

Such termination provisions will usually be triggered if the relevant breach has not been corrected/cured by the service provider within a specified period; 30 calendar days is very much a 'market standard' period in this regard, although we do see shorter periods in some cases (and particularly in the context of contracts which support key trading platforms or which are directly end-customer facing). Some customers also push for an immediate termination right to apply if the relevant material breach is not capable of being cured, but we would caution against reliance upon such a provision in all but the most clear cut of cases (as it would be unfortunate if a customer were to be found to have improperly terminated a contract simply because it thought that the service provider was not able to correct a breach when in fact it was able to do so, albeit over a course of two to three weeks).

A key nuance from a customer perspective is that it will often want the material breach termination right (and indeed many if not all of the other termination rights referred to below) as applying only one way, in its favour, that is, such that the customer has the relevant right of termination, but the service provider does not have the same right in reverse. The customer rationale in this regard is that the impact of a contract termination would be greater for the customer than it would be for the service provider (ie, as all that the supplier is losing is one client, whereas the customer may be losing a key element of support for its business operations), and there should be relatively little that the customer could do wrong that the service provider could not be adequately covered for, either in terms of damages payments and/or by way of the operation of the relief event provisions (see Chapter 7). This has become a common – if not market standard – position on larger scale outsource and managed service style arrangements, although it is less common for public cloud service offerings, and/or regarding on-premise software licence and support arrangements. As such, the only termination right for the service provider may be for non-payment of fees and charges (which we discuss in more detail, below).

An additional aspect of this right that the customer may argue for is to be able to treat a collection or persistent series of breaches which in themselves are not individually materially as being nonetheless a basis for a termination right, if either the breaches are continual/persistent (which would be the more aggressive formulation of the right) and/or which when taken together have a material impact upon the services or the contract as a whole.

2.3 Breach of specified clauses

Any reliance by the customer of the 'material breach' termination provisions set out above carries an inherent degree of risk for the customer, in terms of whether or not a court – in the event of a dispute – would agree not only that the service provider was in breach of contract, but also that the breach was sufficiently serious as to meet the 'material breach' threshold. This cannot be definitively stated in advance, as it has to be viewed in the context of the contract and the underlying deal (such that the bigger and more complex the deal may be, the greater the gravity of the breach would need to be, in order to then justify any purported contract termination).

In order to circumvent this issue, some customers insert additional drafting to the effect that any breach of particular, listed clauses will constitute a potential trigger for termination, no matter how minor or immaterial the breach may be argued to be. Such provisions may for example include any breach of the anti-corruption and bribery provisions or breach of a provision to require completion of services or delivery of defined work products by an absolute, 'drop dead' date (such that time becomes of the essence as at that point). More aggressive formulations of drafting may extend out the list of clauses giving rise to such termination rights so as to include breaches of IT security obligations and/or data protection obligations, or breaches which cause the customer to in turn be in breach of applicable laws and regulations.

2.4 Service level triggers

Many forms of technology and/or long-term service agreements will contain specific service level obligations (see Chapter 4 in this regard). Aside from providing clarity as to the expected levels of service and potentially providing a means for consequential adjustments of the charges by way of the application of service credits, the existence of the service levels may also help the parties to avoid some of the debates as to when a level of poor service has crossed the dividing line between a non-material breach and a material one, by pre-determining this in a more factual (and therefore less open to debate) manner by reference to service level performance.

The common options for the customer to consider in this regard would be:

- breach of the same service level on multiple occasions (eg, more than [X] times in any [Y] consecutive months);
- breach of a (usually particularly important service level) to a significant degree, for example, such that if a key availability related service level was set at 99%, the trigger level for termination might then be much lower, such as at 90%;
- hitting the total amount of service credits put at risk in a given measurement period, either at any point in time (which would be more aggressive) or more than [X] times in any [Y] consecutive months; or
- incurring more than a set percentage of the potentially accruable service credits over a set period of months.

In practice, a combination of the above triggers could be included such that the customer would have the ability to terminate in the event of either persistent/chronic poor service, or more short term but also more serious deteriorations in service quality.

2.5 Required by law/regulation
A customer will be concerned to ensure that it is not tied in to a deal which may in practice be frustrated because it becomes contrary to law or regulation. There are two key possibilities in this regard.

- The provision of the relevant product or services becomes illegal/impermissible by reason of changes in law or regulation which do not relate directly to either party. An obvious example might be where international sanctions come into effect which make the supply of goods or services between entities located in specified countries illegal.
- The provision of the relevant product or services is banned or prevented where a government intercedes to prevent a particular deal proceeding on the grounds of national security or overriding national interests which are linked to where the particular service provider comes from (as we have seen in the technology space in connection with proposed deals with large Chinese players).

In practice, the common law doctrine of frustration would be likely to bring the contract to a close in such circumstances anyway, but the customer will want to avoid any suggestion that the contract might remain on foot (perhaps with the service provider arguing that it is entitled to claim the benefit of relief pursuant to the *force majeure* provisions in the interim), particularly if that would involve it in continuing to make any payments and/or in it being prevented from making alternative arrangements.

2.6 Impact upon reputation

Some customers look beyond the severity of the breach of contract itself, and more towards its end result, particularly *vis-à-vis* their own clients and end-customers. In such circumstances, the customer may seek to insert an express termination right in the event that there was to be an adverse impact upon the customer's reputation within the wider market.

2.7 Termination for convenience/upon notice

In longer-term/multi-year engagements, the customer may in any event want to have the ability to bring the contract to an end simply upon notice to the service provider, and without having to prove any degree of fault. This could for example be because its own needs have changed, or because market conditions have shifted such that the envisaged services are no longer required. Alternatively, it might be involved in some form of merger or acquisition which might entail a re-think of its requirements (for example, if the other entity involved already had a contract in place for the relevant products or services which it could then benefit from in any case).

3. The service provider perspective

The first point to note from the service provider perspective is that while there may not be full mutuality of termination rights, it will want to have as broad a scope of termination rights in its own favour as is possible. Indeed, in some types of contract (such as for public cloud services), the scope of termination rights for the service provider can actually be broader than it is for the customer. The service provider counter-argument to the customer in this regard is that there will be some types of breaches which may not in fact be easily remediable via financial compensation (eg, in relation to breaches of the service provider's intellectual property (IP) rights, or breaches of confidentiality in respect of their proprietary information), and/or that it would in any event be commercially unpalatable for it to be tied in to a continuing relationship with a third party customer who is not respecting their contractual obligations.

We will take each of the proposed termination triggers in turn.

3.1 Insolvency

Clearly the concern of the service provider in the event of a customer insolvency event will be in terms of getting paid, both for work which has already been performed and in relation to any ongoing services which might be required in the future. As such, the service provider will want to argue that any insolvency triggers be made mutual, as the service provider has just as much of an interest to protect in this regard as the customer does.

3.2 Material breach

The service provider concern is ordinarily focused on the time that it will be given to correct the problem before the termination right becomes effective. However, in some contracts (such as public cloud engagements) the service provider may adopt a tougher line, and provide that in the event of there being a material breach which is service delivery related (eg, as opposed to breaches of confidentiality etc), then its first obligation will be to 'use reasonable endeavours' to try to fix the problem – often without there being a specific cure period – and only if it is unable to do so can then either party terminate the contract. However, this will be on the basis that this is then not treated as a 'breach' related termination, and instead the repayment to the customer of any amounts of fees which have been pre-paid for the remainder of the relevant subscription term will be a 'sole and exclusive remedy' for the customer in connection with the termination and the events giving rise to it.

3.3 Breach of specified clauses

The service provider may have its own 'hit list' of sensitive clauses and obligations in this regard. In the context of cloud services which are dependent on infrastructure used to service multiple clients, this may for example include breaches of acceptable use policies (AUPs), on the basis that the customer's breach of those terms would then be potentially impacting upon the service provider's other clients. Other candidates include some that would be of concern to the customer as well (such as the anti-bribery and corruption provisions, or possibly in relation to breaches of the IP/licensing provisions).

However, one specific service provider side termination right which is often seen is a right of termination for non-payment of charges. From a service provider perspective, this is one of the most fundamental obligations that the customer has (if not *the* most fundamental), and it will want to ensure that it can exit from a contract in the event that the customer is not paying for what it is receiving.

3.4 Service level triggers

The service provider will ordinarily want to defer any discussions on service level agreement-related termination rights until such time as the parties have finalised their negotiations on what level the service levels will be set at (on the basis that if they are more challenging for the service provider to achieve, then the risk of the termination rights being triggered will be correspondingly higher). More generally, the service provider will prefer to adopt the position that specific termination triggers linked to the service level agreement regime are not required, on the basis that the customer can in any event rely upon the generic 'material breach' termination right, in the event that the service quality issues are bad enough (albeit in the knowledge that this will always involve an element of doubt/debate as to the degree of 'materiality' involved, such that the service provider will retain a degree of leverage in the commercial discussions which may accompany any threatened exercise of a termination right).

3.5 Required by law/regulation

The service provider will obviously itself not want to be seen as being in breach of contract, in the event that a change in law or regulation actually prevents it from performing (and likewise may not want to have resources tied up in limbo where the contract remains un-performable, but technically still in existence). Accordingly, it may itself want to have a right of termination in such event, and the area of debate will then focus more on the financial consequences of such a termination (as to which, see section 4, below).

3.6 Impact upon reputation

A service provider may well like to get such a termination right, but in practice this is never seen as a termination right in favour of the service provider as opposed to the customer. In fairness, it is much less likely that a default by the customer would give rise to a reputational impact upon the service provider in any event.

3.7 Termination for convenience/upon notice

Likewise, while a service provider would obviously like to have such a right, it is almost unheard of for it to do so (primarily on the basis that it could utilised as a lever to compel the customer to enter into renegotiations, should the service provider determine that it has entered into an unattractive deal, for any reason).

4.   Potential solutions

Before considering the potential compromises in relation to the main termination options as set out above, it is worth noting that the scope of termination rights represents risk from a service provider perspective, which in turn reflects upon the reward it may expect to receive in return. Put simply, therefore, a service provider may be more amenable to a greater breadth of termination provisions, in the event that it is being paid more and/or at a better profit margin.

4.1   Insolvency

It is important to note in this regard that not every insolvency event will necessarily result in the affected party ceasing to be in business; companies may for example go into administration (in the United Kingdom) or Chapter 11 (in the United States) but then be able to restructure and/or obtain new funding, and so continue in business.

From the point of view of potential compromises, a customer could defer a termination right provided that the service provider continues to provide the services etc in a way that does not trigger any other potential termination right. However, the customer will likely want to have some additional comfort in this regard as to what contingency measures that service provider can also take so as to protect business continuity for the customer in the event that the service provider does in fact then slide into oblivion. Options could then include guarantees from parent companies, for example, the service provider may in any event be legally constrained from terminating a contract with a customer who is insolvent. In the United Kingdom, the Insolvency (Protection of Essential Supplies) Order 2015 means that a service provider may not be able to immediately terminate a contract because the customer has been declared insolvent, regardless of what the contract may say. And indeed, it may not actually be the case that the service provider would actually want to terminate, so long as it is still getting paid for its services in the interim. A further option then for the parties to consider would be whether in such cases the service provider's payment profile could be changed such that it is paid in advance rather than in arrears.

4.2   Material breach

The key areas for debate and compromise relate to the period of time for the rectification/cure of any claimed material breaches (the longer the cure period is, the more palatable the termination trigger will be). If there is an additional limb for termination relating to persistent or multiple breaches, the compromise will be to agree that the aggregate impact must have been material, and that the party in breach must have been given reasonable notice not just of the persistent breaches, but also that the terminating party intended to treat them as a basis for termination, were they to continue to occur.

4.3 Breach of specified clauses

Insofar as the parties have agreed upon the list of clauses which may trigger an automatic termination right (ie, without the requirement that the breach of such provisions be 'material' so as to in any event be covered by the more generic material breach termination right), the key areas for discussion regarding potential compromises would be, firstly, the length of the applicable notice and rectification period (which might then for example be longer than the period that would apply for other termination rights), and, secondly, the consequences of the termination (eg, as to whether it would give rise to full or more limited rights of compensation)

4.4 Service level triggers

Similarly with service level agreement-related termination rights, and in particular regarding termination triggers which are linked to persistent poor (but not disastrous) performance rather than more substantial one-off service failures, a potential compromise might be to allow the customer the right of termination, but on the basis that while it may then avoid having to make any form of termination payment as it would do for a termination for convenience (see below), the service provider likewise avoids either some or all of the obligations to make compensation/damages payments, as would otherwise arise following a breach-based contract termination.

Otherwise, the key focus for negotiation will be where the relevant thresholds are set. By way of example, a requirement that a given service level be failed in three consecutive measurement periods is plainly less aggressive/onerous than a trigger which would apply if there were to be three failures in any period of six consecutive months.

4.5 Required by law/regulation

As noted above, both parties have an interest in allowing for a termination where service delivery or receipt is prevented by reason of law or regulation. However, the following different considerations may affect the solutions which the parties may agree in this regard.

- If the legal/regulatory impediment was already in existence when the contract was entered into, the party to whom it relates will likely be seen to be at fault and so liable to compensate the other party.

- If the impediment applied to both parties equally, then it is more likely to be treated more as a termination by reason of *force majeure*, such that the focus will purely be on allocation of costs (as the customer will not be expecting to pay a termination fee as if it were terminating purely for convenience, but the service provider may expect to recover some of its unrecoverable costs and investments up to the date of termination).
- The parties will in any event need to consider (a) whether the impediment affects all of the contract or just part of it; (b) whether the impediment genuinely prevents the contract from being performed or just makes it harder/more expensive to do so; and (c) whether it would be possible to negotiate reasonable amendments so as to circumvent the impact of the relevant law or regulation. In the case of (a), the parties could discuss whether it is possible to sever the affected part of the contract and continue with the rest. For (b), the parties could consider whether it is reasonable for the affected parties to simply bear such costs/added burden, or whether it would be possible to set a threshold to trigger renegotiation and/or a right of termination, if changes could not then be agreed. For (c), the parties could establish an obligation to undertake 'good faith' negotiations to seek to agree a way forward that would avoid the impact of the relevant law or regulation (while recognising that, under English law, such an 'agreement to agree' would not ultimately be enforceable, such that the ultimate termination right would need to remain in place).

4.6 Impact upon reputation

It's more difficult to see a basis for compromise solutions here (other than in relation to the customer potentially agreeing to drop its requirement for this termination trigger in favour of getting its way in terms of some of the other potential termination rights). However, one possibility may be to provide some more specific detail as to what kind of impact there would have to be; for example, in one business process outsourcing (BPO) engagement we were advising on, the termination trigger was linked to the number of customer complaints that were received that were referable to the services being provided by the service provider.

4.7 Termination for convenience/upon notice

The discussions concerning terminations for convenience are almost exclusively driven by commercial considerations.

The service provider perspective will likely be that its pricing was predicated upon getting a certain level/duration of commitment from the customer, such that if the customer choses to step back from that commitment, the service provider should be compensated. The types of compensation that the service provider may then seek to recover will depend on the nature of the deal, but could include:

- either a measure of lost profit for the remainder of the envisaged term or else a clawback of some of the discount that had been provided to the customer (in anticipation of the longer duration) regarding the charges that had accrued prior to the date of termination;
- recovery of as yet unpaid amortised costs;
- unavoidable third-party costs (eg, costs of terminating dedicated third-party contracts or licences);
- employee costs (eg, if customer staff had transferred across under an outsourcing deal and for whatever reason do not then transfer back pursuant to Transfer of Undertakings (Protection of Employment) Regulations 2006 (TUPE)/ Acquired Rights Directive (ARD), and then need to be made redundant); or
- wind-down costs (being a measure of the time costs of service provider personnel during the period that they are rolling-off from the customer's project, and being reassigned to a new one).

Clearly the customer's position will be to try to reduce its exposure to such payments to the greatest extent possible. Options it can consider in this regard may include:

- reducing the level of compensation as the contract continues over time (eg, with a declining amount then being payable to the service provider);
- extending the notice period to be given, again on the basis that less would be payable if the service provider is given greater notice (and so is able to better mitigate its potential costs); or
- obliging the service provider to show how it has used all reasonable endeavours to avoid or mitigate any costs arising as a result of the early termination.

16. Step-in provisions

1. Introduction

Step-in is a mechanism which enables the customer to exert greater levels of direct influence over the services by either taking over the physical performance of the service related task, or by exerting greater management influence over the way in which the services are appointed, or potentially allowing a third party to perform either of these roles on its behalf, requiring the supplier to work alongside the third party.

On the one hand, this is a core part of the customer's ability to be able to correct any underperformance and to ensure that its overall business operation will not be affected. The customer puts its need to receive quality services above everything and this is especially polarised where the customer is a regulated entity that is not permitted to outsource its regulatory compliance such that it will need to take steps to ensure that it is, at any pint, capable of delivering on its regulatory responsibilities, both to regulators and to its customers.

On the other hand, the service provider will be disinclined to allow for interference in its performance, especially where the impact is not significant enough to justify a termination, and will be especially sensitive of allowing step-in in situations impacting upon (or requiring access to) environments used to service its other customers, or situations that would allow a third party (particularly a competitor) to access sensitive material and technology.

2. The customer perspective

At the outset, it is important to note the customer's philosophical motivation behind requiring the inclusion of step-in rights and the desire to activate the rights. As indicated above, the customer will often have assigned or even potentially outsourced a material part of the functional activity of its operations and will be dependent on the provision of the relevant services or outsourcing to be able to continue to carry on as a business. Additionally, it will retain responsibilities both to customers and to regulators to ensure the smooth running of its business in order to deliver a service or to be able to meet its regulatory responsibilities.

This need to ensure continuing operation is the primary motivation from a service provider perspective. Accordingly, it will usually have the view that if there is a service diminution, it will need to take steps to mitigate the impact, and in some circumstances will want to take these steps prior to the event impacting it. But this is not a punishment for the service provider's wrongdoing and it would be wrong to see step-in as a remedy *per se*; step-in is a set of practical activities to facilitate continued operation and does not, in and of itself, generate claims for loss that would then be a sanction for the service provider's behaviour.

2.1 Step-in triggers

As a consequence of the thought process articulated above, the customer will usually argue for a long list of events that, if they occur, give it the right to step-in. These will often include the following circumstances:

- the service provider has committed a breach that has or is likely to cause a material disruption to the performance of the services;
- a certain level of service credits has been accrued, or a certain number of service level defaults have occurred;
- a regulatory requires or recommends that the customer should step in;
- the service provider undergoes a change of control;
- the service provider suffers from an insolvency event;
- the customer has the right to terminate, or either party has issued a right to terminate; or
- the customer has reasonable grounds to suspect any of the above circumstances is more likely than not to occur.

Of particular importance to regulated entities will the ability to be able to step-in when it is necessary to do so from a regulatory entity. Regulatory regimes, especially in the financial services sector, are especially clear that regulated entities cannot outsource compliance with regulatory functions and must maintain an approved level of oversight and influence in relation to the outsourced activities and that they must take appropriate action if the service provider may not be carrying out the tasks effectively.

Moreover, because the purpose of the step-in is to mitigate and avoid impact on the performance of the services, the customer may well argue that it should have the ability to step-in on a pre-emptive basis, for example, when it has reasonable grounds to suspect one of the other step-in rights will occur. This can, however, be particularly problematic for a service provider, if it believes that it is in a good position to resolve the relevant concerns before they do, in fact, impact upon the customer (and especially if the exercise of the step-in rights would have an adverse commercial impact upon the service provider).

2.2 What steps the customer can take when stepping-in

The customer will ask for the ability to take whatever steps it requires to ensure that the services are provided in accordance with the terms of the agreement, and this usually has two specific elements. First, the ability to 'take over', either in replacement of or in conjunction with, the service provider of the affected services and secondly, the ability to provide more definitive management oversight and direction, and to issue instructions with which the service provider must comply. Most probably, the customer will want to extend these rights to a third party appointed to act on its behalf, particularly when the customer itself does not possesses the requisite skills and experience to perform effectively the relevant tasks.

As part of the exercise of these rights, the customer would expect that the service provider will provide the assistance required by the customer or the third party appointed on its behalf so that the step-in rights can be properly effected, and will likely want to be clear that the rights to use software, systems, materials etc, provided by the service provider are extended for the purposes of properly carrying out the step-in. Not having these rights would, in the customer's mind, materially hamstring its ability to exercise the step-in rights, and to achieve the practical objectives.

2.3 What is the duration of the step-in?

From a customer point of view, the answer to this question will likely be: as long as is required to 'steady the ship' so that the customer is comfortable that the services will, on an on-going basis, be provided in accordance with the terms of the agreement. Ultimately, however, most customers recognise that step-in for an elongated period is not a palatable or effective long-term solution to service issues. It would be usual, therefore, for the customer to expect that if it has not 'stepped out' after a certain period of time, the agreement would instead either terminate, or switch back to allow the service provider to take back control.

Many customers will argue that a termination in this situation is not one that it wanted to generate; and that it is occurring only because the service provider has either been at fault in the first instance or has not been able to remediate the step-in situation such that the customer should step-out. As a consequence of this argument, the customer will likely require the termination as a result of a lengthy step-in period to be a termination by reason of the service provider's breach.

2.4 Cost consequences of step-in

The customer will incur its own internal costs of stepping-in and will incur the costs of a third party. It will not, therefore, be willing to incur what it considers to be duplicative costs by also paying the service provider the charges calculated in accordance with the agreement for providing services it is not providing. Accordingly, the customer will want to include a provision that suspends payment of the charges related to the functions which are subject to the step-in rights for the duration of the step-in events.

The customer will also seek that its costs of step-in be reimbursed by the service provider, and also potentially any broader losses it has incurred. This is a justifiable perspective because, even though the exercise of a step-in right is not a punishment, had the service provider properly complied with its broader responsibility under the agreement (such as the performance of obligations in accordance with service standards, or compliance with service levels etc) the customer really ought not to have had to exercise the right. As such, it is reasonable for these costs and losses to sit with the service provider.

2.5 Step-out

Before being prepared to step-out, and allow the service provider to recommence performance of the services, the customer will want to be assured that the issue generating the reason to step-in has been either eradicated or sufficiently mitigated to mean that the Services will now be performed in accordance with the terms of the agreement.

In this respect, the customer will expect the service provider to prepare, for the customer's approval, a step-out plan that articulates the steps the service provider has undertaken in order to address the underlying issues, together with the date on which the service provider believes the customer should step-out and the supplier steps back in to perform. It will be important from the customer's point of view that it controls the step-out process so as not to undo the effort and costs incurred in exercising the right to step-in over the preceding weeks or even months.

Once the customer has approved the step-out plan, the service provider will be expected to implement a more detailed version of it and to enable the customer to monitor its performance in respect of it.

3.   The service provider perspective

The service provider has been appointed to provide the services in some respects precisely because it offers a better service than the customer is able to provide for itself (or has an offering which the customer cannot replicate) and is more skilled and experienced in the performance of the relevant tasks. Accordingly, enabling and facilitating a situation whereby the customer is able to take over the provision of the services is unusual to say the least and, in many circumstances, simply not appropriate. Additionally, a large part of sourcing engagements, especially cloud-based solutions, leverage shared staff, environments and material, together with the service provider's proprietary methodologies and intellectual property (IP) that it simply cannot (for fear of impact on other customers) or will not (because of the competitively advantageous nature of them) permit third parties to access.

The exercise of a step-in right is fraught with so many difficult issues that the customer should view it as akin to a right to terminate, and should either assume similar circumstances as that which occur with the right to terminate, or, rely on its rights to terminate instead.

If the service provider is prepared to allow step-in, the following will likely form part of its approach to the provisions.

3.1   Step-in triggers

The ability on the part of the customer to step-in should be very carefully controlled because of the impact it can have on the performance of the services, not just during the step-in period but on a potentially longer-term basis thereafter. Consequently, the customer ought only to have the ability to step-in where the service provider has actually defaulted under the agreement and, potentially, in recognition of the regulatory constraints under which a customer operates, if a regulator specifically requires the customer to step-in.

Of the other scenarios envisaged by a customer, it is not necessary for these to be specifically identified as they will be caught by a right to step-in where the service provider has committed a material breach or would not in and of themselves necessarily point to the service provider not performing in accordance with the terms of the agreement (eg with regards to the service of a notice of termination or the service provider having undergone a change of control) such that they do not justify a right to terminate in any event.

As an additional step, a supplier will, as with a termination for breach scenario, anticipate being afforded a period of time in which to remediate the circumstances that are giving rise to the right to step-in. This will be a reasonable middle step-in order to prevent the customer from having to exercise the right and incur the trouble in doing so, while also protecting the service provider from inappropriate and knee-jerk reactions.

3.2 The steps that can be taken as part of the step-in

Because of the challenges associated with allowing a customer to step-in to service delivery centres that are used to provide services to third parties, the service provider's view will be that step-in can involve only the service provider working in conjunction with a third party appointed by the customer in an effort to investigate and address any service related issues. It cannot involve the actual performance of takes by the customer itself or a third party.

Additionally, the service provider might well be unwilling to allow a competitor to have a measure of detailed insight into its operations and ways of working as this would of course create an unfair impact on its ability to operate in the market, and potentially provide that competitor with an unreasonable level of advantage. As such, the third party should not be a competitor, or if it is, would need to be subject to direct confidentiality agreements with the supplier and would not, in any event, be permitted to access any proprietary material.

3.3 Responsibility for the step-in and impact on the agreement

If the service provider is in fact not providing the services or is being required to follow the customer's (or its appointed third party's instructions) it would not be reasonable, in the service provider's opinion, for the supplier to retain the same level of responsibility for the performance of the relevant services. It is no longer performing the services under its own determination and therefore it should not be reasonable for it to bear the consequences (including any knock-on impact upon such of the contracted-for services which it is still providing). The service provider will likely want this position to be articulated within the step-in provisions. Moreover, there is a reasonable chance that the exercise of the step-in could have some longer-term impacts on the service provider's ability to perform in accordance with the terms of the agreement, especially the service levels, and so will expect an express relief to be provided in these circumstances. If the exercise of the step-in right means that the service provider incurs additional costs in the performance of the services when it recommences them, it would expect the customer to bear these additional costs, as these are all consequent on the customer's own acts and omissions (although this may depend on whether the step-in action results from a demonstrable breach of contract by the service provider).

3.4 Duration of the step-in

In the same way as the service provider might seek to require the customer to exercise a right to terminate the agreement rather than step-in, it will usually require there to be a definitive limit on the duration of the step-in period, so as to allow for some finality to both the step-in situation and any broader issues related to service performance. A step-in is disruptive to the service provider's ability to manage the account and it would rather have the customer terminate than be exposed to a lengthy and uncertain period of step-in.

As such, the customer should commit to limiting the period of step-in to as long as is strictly necessary and, in any event, a defined period, probably not to exceed two months. At the end of this period, the customer should automatically step-out, and if it refuses to do so, this should be deemed to bring the agreement to an end (with the consequences of termination then being judged by reference to whatever circumstances had triggered the step-in rights in the first place). While this might make it appear that the service provider is forfeiting the charges payable under the deal, this imperative on the part of the customer to step-out or go through a difficult exit and reprocurement exercise will, for many service providers, act as a clear leverage for the customer to bring the step-in to an end and permit the service provider to take back the services.

3.5 Commercial consequences of step-in

So far, we have dealt with the service provider's point of view when it comes to the ramifications of the step-in exercise. Associated with that set of terms, is the impact on the charges during the step-in period. As we saw above, the customer will expect not to pay the charges and the service provider to compensate it for at least the third-party costs incurred in the step-in. Conversely, if the service provider is in fact still providing support (even if not the full scope of services) or is likely to be required to recommence performance on short notice, it will expect to continue to be paid so that it is fairly compensated for its effort and can guarantee the availability of resources and staff at the point of step-out.

It would not be expected that the customer would compensate for the costs incurred unless the reason for step-in was clearly a result of the service provider's breach of the agreement, and even then the service provider would expect a limitation (probably by reference to a percentage of the charges ordinarily payable to it for the relevant affected services) on its responsibility to reimburse so that the customer would not incur an inappropriate level of costs, under the assumption that whatever it incurs the service provider will incur. It would be reasonable for the customer to play a role in limiting these costs and this can be achieved by placing a limitation on the supplier's exposure to them.

3.6   Step-out
As indicated earlier, the service provider will expect the customer to step-out after a relatively short period of step-in. In this regard, then, it will be the customer that will step-out in order to allow the suppler to recommence performance. The onus will therefore be on the customer to affect the step-out in an orderly manner, rather than for the service provider to generate a step-out plan, and to put this into effect with the customer's approval.

4.   Potential solutions
In large part the solutions that might apply to the challenges presented by these polarised views on step-in can largely be overcome by understanding and dealing with the commercial consequences of the step-in. Addressing the consequences, or lack thereof, from a liability and payment point of view will usually unlock the difficulty in negotiating these provisions.

4.1   Step-in triggers
In the first instance, it is essential to understand the nature of the agreement and whether it lends itself to step-in. For example, solutions heavily predicated on cloud services or that do not affect important functions (whether from a business perspective or regulatory standpoint) are unlikely to justify a full set of step-in provisions. Accordingly, a better approach in these situations will be to address issues via enhanced monitoring, the provision of

third-party support that the service provider must work with and appropriate remediation plans, while understanding the Plan B for the service, in the extreme circumstances which might ordinarily give rise to step-in considerations.

Where step-in is appropriate, the triggers can often be aligned to the customer's initial view point on the express understandings that:

- the service provider has the ability to demonstrate that the step-in right is not necessary and that the customer will be reasonable in forming a view as to the validity of this remedial plan; and
- where the right to step-in is taken other than where the service provider is actually at fault, the commercial consequences of this, for example, in relation to third-party costs, will be absorbed by the customer. Accordingly, the customer is afforded the practical solution it seeks but on the basis that it might need to bear material costs, which will often act as a disincentive to take the steps or at least will be a checkpoint for it to ensure it really wants to exercise the right to step-in.

4.2 The steps that can be taken during step-in

It is in this area that the most material compromises can be reached, with a recognition of the appropriate limitations of interfering in operations used to support other clients.

It is relatively normal that a customer is not permitted to step-in to those elements of its operations and service delivery model that is genuinely sued to provide services to third parties, for fear that this would potentially create a liability for the supplier with regard to its other customers. This is usually accepted by customers so long as there is a level of genuine use for third parties, and on the basis that the supplier commits that it will not allow other third parties to exercise similar step-in rights. Consequently, the right to step-in moves away from a form of physical self-performance, to management oversight, potentially supported by expert third parties. Additionally, if volume can be diverted away from the service provider to an alternative service delivery model (eg, the business continuity arrangements) this can be an additional mode of solving the actual performance challenges.

4.3 Duration of step-in

Regularly, an absolute limit will be agreed on the duration of the step-in, with the associated proviso that at the end of the step-in period the customer will either step-out and allow the service provider to start to perform, or will terminate the agreement, often for the same reason for which it stepped-in in the first instance (and without prejudice to any other rights as may have accrued in the meantime).

4.4 Commercial consequences of step-in

If the reason for the step-in is the service provider's default, it would usually be expected to bear the commercial consequences, albeit potentially applying a cap as described in the service provider arguments section above, and again without prejudice to the customer's right to claim for other losses that may be incurred. Where the customer decides to step-in based on no-fault situations or on an anticipatory basis, the costs will usually lie where they fall (unless the anticipated reason for the step-in is the service provider's default and this does subsequently occur, in which case the supplier would usually bear the costs). The service provider may (reasonably) want to insert an express obligation upon the customer to act reasonably in this regard and to mitigate its exposure where possible to do so (which is likely to be no more than a reflection of what English law would require in any event, although other jurisdictions may differ).

17. Audit rights

1. **Introduction**

Many forms of technology services arrangements can be said to be critical to the operation of the customer's business. This is certainly the case in relation to some of the wider scoped outsourcing contracts, where large proportions of the customer's IT, telecoms and/or other business operations may end being entrusted to the care of the service provider. However, even in the case of more limited scope arrangements or services, what the service provider does may still be of significant importance to the customer and its compliance with its own legal and contractual obligations. Indeed, many software-related offerings or software as a service (SaaS) offerings can be absolutely critical to how the customer operates, interacts with its end clients and regulators, and/or organises its internal affairs.

Accordingly, while the customer may take some degree of comfort from whatever forms of contractual protection and sanctions it has been able to negotiate with the service provider in relation to the proper performance of the relevant services, that may very well not be enough to allow it to sleep soundly at night. It is certainly always better to be proactive and to be able to spot potential issues and stop them developing into problems, rather than have such problems arise and then seek to recover compensation or apply other sanctions against the service provider. It is in this context, therefore, that audit rights have to be considered.

An audit right would typically therefore involve an ability for a customer to have access to documentation, systems, premises and/or personnel involved with the provision of the relevant services, so as to enable the customer to assess them and assure itself that everything is as it should be, and that the provisions of the relevant contract are being complied with. This sounds straightforward enough, but in practice such provisions can often be subject to fierce negotiation and indeed can be rejected outright by some service providers, particularly if the services in question involve the use of common systems, premises or infrastructure across multiple end clients, such that the practical exercise of an audit right may not be as straightforward as one might have first assumed.

In this chapter, therefore, we look at the various different component parts of an audit related provision in turn, and consider the customer and service provider perspectives in relation to each one.

2. The customer perspective

2.1 Frequency

Ideally, the customer would want to be able to conduct audits as often and whenever it would like. In relation to functions which have been outsourced in particular, the customer may point to the fact that had it retained the relevant operations in-house, it would have been able to have conduct reviews of them whenever it wanted to, and so would not want the position to be any different once the functions have been entrusted to the service provider.

2.2 Scope

In a similar vein, the customer will ideally want to touch upon everything and anything which relates to the provision of the relevant services; the customer will, accordingly, want to have the scope of the permitted audit to be worded as widely as possible, and ideally to be delineated primarily by reference to its discretion as to what it decides it wants to inspect or to see. This will, therefore, be likely to include:

- documentation relating to the provision of the services;
- customer data (ie, copies of the customer's own data which may be in the service provider's possession or control); and/or
- access to the premises and systems which are utilised to provide the services (so as to check that they are in conformance with the relevant requirements of the agreement, for example as to security arrangements).

2.3 Conditions

The customer's concern in this regard is to ensure that its ability to carry out its intended audit is not frustrated by reason of the application of conditions (eg, by the service provider insisting upon compliance with security protocols which are so convoluted or time consuming that the customer is effectively prevented from being able to carry out a 'snap' check, if that is what is intended, or requiring that the customer and/or its auditors sign up to unspecified confidentiality or policy compliance related agreements).

Accordingly, the customer will want to have as few conditions or requirements attached to the audit process as possible, and any conditions as are to be set would ideally be exhaustively recorded in the contract. It is also worth noting in this regard that customers, for example, in the financial services sector may also be subject to additional pressures in this regard from their regulators. If we look at the European Banking Association (EBA) guidelines on outsourcing, we will see that they refer to a requirement for 'unrestricted' access and audit rights, and a requirement to ensure that the contractual arrangements "do not impede or limit the effective exercise of access and audit rights". On that basis, the customer may argue that the contract should not contain any potential fetters on its audit rights at all.

2.4 Auditors

The customer may have the resource and expertise itself to carry out an audit of its service providers. However, it is more likely that it will need some help in this regard, and in particular may need the freedom to engage some specialists who will be able to assist it in ascertaining whether things are in fact as they should be (both in terms of what the contract requires and by reference to business practices more generally). The customer would, accordingly, want the contract to specifically allow it to appoint agents or contractors to assist it with the audit process, or to undertake the audit on its behalf.

2.5 Cost

Audits can potentially be time consuming and costly processes (and the larger and more complex the audited services are, the more lengthy and costly the associated audit will likely be). The customer will ordinarily be happy to bear the costs of undertaking the audit with respect of its own efforts and in terms of paying the costs of any external party it engages to assist with it (as discussed above), but may want to provide that these costs will be borne by the service provider in the event that the audit were to reveal any misfeasance or contractual defaults on the part of the service provider.

The service provider may also incur some level of costs in connection with the audit (eg, if it has to spend time in gathering information requested during the audit process, or to devote time from its personnel to assist with the audit more generally). However, the customer will argue that this should have been costed into the project charges and estimates by the service provider at the outset, such that such assistance should be considered to be a part of the core services and so not be chargeable in addition to them.

2.6 Liability

There is always the possibility that an audit may cause some disruption either to the provision of the services or even to the service provider's other operations. However, the customer will likely prefer the contract to be silent on this point, and to simply have the undertaking of the audit to be subject to the general provisions of the contract (including as to relevant liability limits etc).

2.7 Consequences

As noted above, the customer will want to provide that if it has had to undertake an audit in order to uncover some wrongful acts or omissions on the part of the service provider, then it should not have to bear any costs associated with the audit and the service provider should pay for it instead.

Moreover, the customer may also want to then include an express obligation upon the service provider to promptly undertake whatever remedial actions are required by any report as may be produced at the end of the audit process (with the potential addition of a breach termination right if it fails to do so within a specified period).

3. The service provider perspective

3.1 Frequency

The key concern of the service provider in connection with audits is the potential disruption that they cause to its operations, both on behalf of the customer and potentially in relation to its other clients as well. As such, if audits are to be permitted at all, it is in the service provider's interests to have them as infrequently as possible, and so the service provider may argue that the audit should only take place in the event that there is a legal or regulatory obligation upon the customer to undertake such an audit.

3.2 Scope

For the same disruption related reasons, the service provider will want the audit to be as limited in scope as possible, and in particular it will want it to exclude any potential aspects of its premises or systems as are not directly related to the provision of services to the particular customer, and to the particular project which is the subject of the relevant audit. The service provider may therefore seek to restrict the audit just to the inspection of specified categories of documentation (eg, supporting materials for submitted invoices), to those parts of its premises as may be exclusively dedicated to the provision of the services to the particular customer, and/or to systems or software which are similarly dedicated exclusively to the customer. The service provider will be particularly keen to ensure that the scope of the audit specifically excludes:

- systems, infrastructure or parts of its premises which are also used to service other clients;
- any documentation or systems which may include information or data relating to other clients; and/or
- any material which may be commercially confidential to the service provider, including, in particular, internal audit reports of the service provider itself and any underlying price related information which might then disclose the service provider's profit margins.

The service provider may also be wary of audits which are potentially being used as fishing expeditions in the context of potential disputes; a savvy service provider may therefore also retain the right to disapply the audit rights in the context of any contractual dispute as may have arisen between the parties.

3.3 Conditions

The service provider will argue that it has legitimate concerns as to the manner in which any audit may be conducted, such that it would be reasonable for it to require compliance with certain specified conditions. Such preconditions may include compliance with the service provider's applicable premises and security policies, or to require that any access to its premises or systems be accompanied and supervised by members of the service provider's own staff, so as to make sure that the agreed scope of the audit is not exceeded and that any information regarding other clients is not endangered.

3.4 Auditors

Audits can be potentially far reaching affairs which would involve disclosure of a lot of information which the service provider may see as being commercially confidential, even if related to the provision of services to the customer. As such, the service provider will be wary about any such information coming into the hands of one of its competitors. For example, if a project has involved a particularly novel or inventive process or way of working, the service provider will obviously not want this to then be disclosed to or pored over by one of its competitors, if such a competitor has been engaged by the customer to carry out the audit on its behalf. As such, the service provider may want the appointment of any third-party auditor to be subject to its consent, or to expressly exclude any entity which would be considered to be a competitor of the service provider (which the service provider would ideally want to be able to determine in its own discretion or leave open for future interpretation, given the fact that who may be or become a competitor of the service provider may change during the lifetime of the contract in question).

3.5   Cost

Given the time and effort that can be involved in assisting with and facilitating an audit, the service provider will be concerned about the potential drain upon its resources; after all, if it has continuing service delivery obligations to the customer which will continue to need to be met, any time spent in resolving audit related queries may be at the cost of having to 'back fill' the service delivery functions in the meantime. Notwithstanding the customer perspective on this point as discussed above, the service provider will likely argue that it is not practicable for it to pre-estimate the amount of effort that might be involved in this regard, not least because it will not know in advance how many times the customer may invoke its audit rights, nor necessarily know how extensive and intrusive the audits may then end up being, or how much 'hand holding' the audit team may require. Accordingly – and also as a way of discouraging the customer from over-exercising such audit rights as may be available to it – the service provider will argue that it should be entitled to be paid for all of the assistance that it is required to provide to the conduct of the audit.

3.6   Liability

The service provider view here is that while the customer may choose to undertake an audit, it does not have to do so (save potentially in the context of heavily regulated sectors such as the public sector or in financial services). Accordingly, the service provider may take the view that if the customer or those acting on its behalf do something wrong in the conduct of the audit and thereby cause the service provider some loss (eg, by inadvertently disrupting the operation of systems which also support other clients), then the customer should be responsible for such costs/losses (and ideally on an unlimited and/or indemnity basis).

3.7 Consequences

The service provider will likely find it difficult to argue that it should not be obliged to rectify any contractual non-compliances which the audit may have uncovered. However, there is then the question of the costs of the audit. Audit exercises may be extensive, time consuming and (therefore) somewhat expensive. The service provider may therefore argue that if the customer was going to undertake such an audit in any event (eg, as part and parcel of its standard outsourcing policy, or as part of its standard approach to vendor management), then such costs of the audit should be always borne by the customer, and the service provider's sole liability should be in respect of the rectification of any discrepancies that the audit may have uncovered.

4. Potential solutions

4.1 Frequency

In practice, the customer will likely have neither the time nor the inclination to undertake multiple audits in any given year. In normal circumstances, therefore, having some limitations on the frequency of audits may be acceptable, provided that the provisions also take account of the 'unknown unknowns', which may therefore give rise to a need to undertake an additional audit activity, outside the normally agreed frequency. The parties may accordingly agree for audits to be permissible:

- where required by law or by a regulator with jurisdiction or authority over the operations of the customer;
- where there is a reasonable suspicion of a material breach on the part of the service provider in relation to its contractual obligations (or perhaps specifically if there is suspicion of IT security or personal data related breaches, given the higher risk profile and sensitivity related to them); or
- [X] times in a defined period, usually a calendar year or consecutive 12-month period.

4.2 Scope

It seems reasonable for a service provider to want to preclude any audit impacting upon (or requiring the disclosure of data relating to) its other clients; after all, the customer would not want the service provider to be agreeing audit terms with those other clients which could allow for the possibility of impact upon the customer's own data or operations. However, where there are parts of premises which would reasonably need to be accessed in the context of an audit operation which are not entirely devoted to the customer, it may suffice for the audit access to be accompanied/supervised by service provider personnel, who can then ensure that there is no inadvertent disclosure of any materials which do not relate directly to the customer.

4.3 Conditions

It seems reasonable enough that anyone connected with the audit should be under appropriate obligations of confidentiality, but rather than requiring new/separate non-disclosure agreements or confidentiality agreements to be negotiated/put in place, a compromise solution may be to have the customer take on an obligation to ensure that any third parties that it engages to assist with the audit abide by the same obligations of confidentiality that it has under the terms of the relevant agreement, and to therefore be responsible for any breaches of confidentiality by them (which, as per Chapter 13, will often be expressed on an unlimited liability basis). The customer can then protect itself by ensuring that it includes mirror image confidentiality obligations in its contract with whoever it then engages to undertake the audit activities.

If there are any other obligations or conditions to be imposed, then they should be stated explicitly in the contract and agreed up front, that is, such that both parties are comfortable with their terms, and the audit will not then be capable of being frustrated by reason of a failure to agree upon uncertain conditions in future.

4.4 Auditors

The concerns of the service provider as to who may conduct an audit have a lot of validity, both as to the risk of misuse of confidential information and the inherent risk of a degree of impartiality (as an auditor who is also a competitor of the service provider may have a temptation or inclination to take a more negative slant of what it sees during the course of the audit). However, the customer may equally point out that if the nature of the audit is such that it needs to address highly technical issues (eg, as to compliance with technical specifications or security obligations and so on), then the competence or skill set to carry out the audit may be in relatively short supply, such that the customer in effect has no choice but to engage someone who the service provider might conceivably consider to be a competitor.

The solution to this issue may come about through a combination of factors:

- addressing the obligations of confidentiality to be placed upon any third-party auditor, as already discussed above;
- providing that any auditor be accompanied/supervised by the service provider itself; and/or
- either limiting any 'black list' competitors to a short, defined list of key competitors (such that the customer still has a reasonable number of choices of other entities to appoint), or else taking the alternative approach and setting out a 'white list' of entities who the customer can select from in order to carry out the audit (eg, the likes of PwC, KPMG, EY and Deloitte are often mentioned by reason of their historic links to their audit practices, their consulting capabilities and the perception that they are beholden to professional duties of confidentiality in any event).

4.5 Cost

If the service provider has bid for a project knowing that the customer has got a right to undertake a minimum number of audits per year, then there may be an argument for saying that it should have factored the assumed cost of assisting with such an audit in its pricing, such that there would then be no possibility of raising any additional charges for such minimum audits. Under that model, the service provider would however then be able to levy a charge for additional audits that the customer undertakes beyond the set minimum number (at least subject to the point below regarding liability).

It may however be argued by the service provider that it either hasn't done this in practice, or else that it may not be in the customer's interests for it to do so if the customer itself is not absolutely wedded to doing the minimum number of audits, come what may (as the customer might end up bearing an assumed cost of an audit which does not then in fact take place). In such cases, a compromise may be to offer to pay some fixed/discounted amount to the service provider, each time that a standard audit takes place (but not then in relation to audits which arise by reason of anticipated/suspected breaches which are then found to have arisen – see below).

4.6 Liability

The customer can in all likelihood accept that it would be reasonable for it to at least try not to cause any disruption to the service provider's operations and provision of services to its other clients. In that regard, the customer may therefore be willing to accept liability for loss/damage caused by the customer as a result of any negligent act or omission on its part (or the part of its third-party auditor) during the audit process. However, the customer may not wish to have such liability expressed as being either on an indemnity basis, nor for the liability to be unlimited. While the service provider may remain nervous about the potential consequences of the actions of the customer or its auditor (eg, the potential of disruption to multiple clients and therefore multiple claims for compensation, etc), it may become more comfortable about such risks if the audit provisions build in some of the other compromise positions referred to in this chapter, and in particular the ability to escort and monitor the activities of the auditors (which may then help prevent any potential issues arising).

4.7 Consequences

The key question here is the proportion of the audit costs that should be borne by the service provider, in circumstances where the audit has uncovered some breaches of contract on its part.

Given that the service provider may have little control over the scope of the audit or the identity of the auditor (depending on what has otherwise been agreed, as per the issues flagged in this chapter), and/or the terms and payments which the customer has negotiated with the third-party auditor, options for consideration include:

- setting a cap on the amount that the service provider can be obliged to contribute towards the costs of the audit;
- providing that the service provider will not be obliged to pay for the costs of the audit unless any defects in performance/contract obligations uncovered by the audit are 'material'; or
- linking the amount of the contribution of the service provider to a sliding scale, depending on the gravity/cost of rectification of the underlying issues.

18. Dispute resolution provisions

1. Introduction

It ought to be in both parties' interests to resolve, as practicably as possible, any significant debates or disputes that arise in connection with the performance of a technology services agreement, and particularly so in respect of a long-term agreement where the parties may otherwise find themselves deadlocked in some kind of 'deadly embrace'. Resolution of disputes should ideally be done in a structured way, and in a timely manner, so that the parties can get back to the primary objective of the agreement: namely to provide and receive service to make a profit, on the part of the service provider, and support its broader business objectives on the part of the customer.

In many cases, the negotiation of the dispute resolution provisions is indeed straightforward. There are, however, some particular challenges if one party favours a particular style of resolution, especially if this is not offered or expected to be agreed on a genuinely symmetrical basis.

2. The customer perspective

The customer will usually want to be able to control the choice of the dispute resolution mechanism, on the basis that the disputes will likely relate to the quality of the services it receives and that support its business and the charges it is expected to pay. The primary options available to it in this regard are as set out below.

2.1 Escalation

The primary source of dispute escalation will be via an escalation process within both of the service provider and customer organisations by references to tiers of increasing seniority of management, in a timeboxed fashion. The issues that most usually arise are the period of time taken at each level of the escalation process, and the identity or the roles of the individuals who must be involved at each of the levels.

2.2   Mediation and arbitration

If a dispute remains unresolved after escalation, the next stage will usually be to enter into a process of mediation, whereby an appointed third party will mediate structured negotiations between the parties in an effort to reach a negotiated settlement. Again, given there are industry bodies with established reputations and processes relating to the conduct of negotiations then, so long as the parties can agree on the body's rules to be followed, this does not tend to be contentious.

Similarly, if the parties choose arbitration over courts, it is usually because they prefer any combination of:

- the greater confidentiality afforded to disputes handled via arbitration;
- the subject matter expertise of the arbitrators; and/or
- a wish to avoid challenges with enforcing judgments in countries where reciprocal enforcement treaties do not exist.

Then, provided the relevant body can be agreed upon, it is relatively straightforward to conclude in negotiations.

2.3   Referral to courts

The involvement of courts in dispute resolution appears in two instances. Most significantly, where courts are chosen as the ultimate dispute resolution forum instead of arbitration, and, secondly where, notwithstanding the parties being engaged in a dispute resolution process, the parties wish to reserve their rights to go to court to enforce rights in any event.

The customer will of course want to ensure that the choice of court will be one with which it is comfortable, and specifically will not be one that affords to the supplier any 'home court' advantage, if the service provider is located in a different jurisdiction from it.

One area that can be more contentious is the ability of the customer to refer disputes to court, as it sees fit, irrespective of the outcome of a dispute resolution process. The customer will seek this right in order to make sure that it does not become embroiled in negotiations where the service provider is not, in its opinion, seeking to engage proactively in the discussions or in order to make sure that it does not lose any legal rights or suffer any detriment as a consequence of failing to enforce such legal rights as it might have.

The customer will often seek that this is a unilateral right for its benefit only, on the basis that it is essential to protect its intellectual property (IP), confidential information, ability to continue to do business in the market place and to protect itself from paying significant sums of money from undue charges. It will often believe it is not relevant for the service provider to have equivalent rights because the risks it needs to protect are materially smaller than those of the customer, given that the customer is not in a position to undermine the service provider's business operations in the same way a supplier can do with a customer.

2.4 Ability to appoint an expert

Often the customer will feel at a disadvantage to the service provider because of its lack of understanding or visibility in terms of the scope of the services and the manner in which the service provider provides the services. Even with appointing a strong team of advocates, its ability to argue its case properly will inevitably be limited by reason of this lack of knowledge.

As such, it would be a sensible option for customers to have the right to appoint an expert as an arbiter in relation to disputes, especially those of a technical or operational nature. The customer may feel that this ought to be a right solely for the customer given this lack of understanding and the relative disadvantage. It should be for the customer to determine the identity of the expert as it will be likely to be less capable of influencing market participants, as experts will likely be, and should be, the party that formally appoints the expert.

The customer will anticipate that the expert's decision on technical matters will be binding on the supplier, on the basis that it has appointed the service provider.

2.5 Beneficiaries and herding of claims

Most entities that enter into at least moderately complicated outsourcing agreements will be part of a group of entities, and the customer will often be a contracting representative of that entire group. It will, therefore, be essential that the members of the customer group have the ability to enforce the terms of the agreement as if they were the contracting entity, because the agreement is as much for their benefit as any other company within the group.

In the customer's opinion, it is necessary for the group members to be able to enforce on their own behalf for a variety of reasons, including:
- the actual level of control the entities within the group have over each other;
- the possibility of a court declining that one entity has the ability to bring claims on behalf of another;

- the practical difficulties in bringing claims on behalf of others, such as the location of witnesses, accounting practices etc; and/or
- the additional costs involved in multi-party litigation.

3. The service provider perspective

As indicated above, many elements of the dispute resolution process do not tend to attract significant areas of negotiation. Where they do, they can lead to emotive discussions if the perception is that one party is seeking to prevent another from enforcing its contractual rights.

3.1 Referral to courts

The service provider will expect to have the ability to refer the protection of at least its IP and confidential information to the courts in any circumstance, on the basis there is little, if any, justification for treating this any differently from that belonging to the service provider. If there is any suggestion that the customer is in breach of the IP or confidentiality provisions, the service provider should have the ability to enforce these terms as rapidly as possible.

3.2 Ability to appoint an expert

From the service provider's perspective, either the appointment forms part of the structured escalation process or the parties must agree on the referral of the dispute to an expert. If an expert is to be appointed, then it must be on the basis of a joint appointment given the varying expertise of experts, and the need for both parties to provide input to the expert in order for him or her to provide an appropriate and fair result. Specifically, because of the client's perceived lack of expertise, it would be necessary for the service provider to be involved in the process in order to make sure their consideration does not veer off course.

3.3 Beneficiaries and herding of claims

While it might be acceptable for the contract to recognise that the ultimate benefit of the agreement is provided to the contracting customer's affiliates, the service provider may assert that it is not appropriate for the affiliates to have the ability to bring direct claims for a variety of reasons including:

- the indirect nature of the claims and the likelihood this will give rise to a broader nature of liability;

- the lack of a day to day connection with the affiliate which will increase their propensity to bring a claim; and/or
- the proliferation risk, whereby dealing with multiple claims will increase its risk profile and cost and expenses of handling various claims.

Accordingly, the service provider would argue that it would not be acceptable for affiliates to bring their own claims, and instead the claims must be brought via the contracting customer entity.

The service provider would thus argue that the customer must procure that the affiliates do not bring any claims on their own behalf, and provide an indemnity in favour of the service provider on an unlimited basis if they do. The reason for this indemnity is because of the nature of the claims. If a group entity brings a claim it will likely do so in tort which might therefore sit outside the agreement. As it is a non-contractual claim it will not be subject to the limits on liability, and will therefore exponentially expose the service provider to a level of unlimited liability that would never have occurred had the customer's affiliates not brought these claims. It is possible for the customer to stop these claims and bring the claims on behalf of its affiliates and it should do so.

4. Potential solutions

As can be seen from the commentary above, the main issues regarding dispute resolution relate to two areas:

- referral to courts; and/or
- claims from affiliates.

4.1 Referral to courts

The principal way of resolving this area is for each party to have the ability to refer to courts its right to enforce its entitlement to protection of its IP or confidential information. Potentially this can be preceded with a short remediation period, if that is considered appropriate.

4.2 Beneficiaries and herding of claims

Generally, it is recognised that a contract is being entered into by one entity on behalf of a group, and that accordingly, these group members should not be left out of pocket should they incur a loss as a consequence of the supplier's breach of the agreement. The usual compromise is to allow the affiliate to bring its claims only after the primary customer entity has tried to bring the claims or where the contracting customer entity is prevented from bringing an effective claim.

As such, the affiliates would be permitted to bring claims directly where:

- the primary customer contracting entity has failed at first instance as a consequence of not having sufficient standing to bring the claim;
- the relevant procedural rules or applicable laws prohibit them from bringing the claims; or
- the contracting customer entity would, in the professional opinion of a leading independent lawyer, not be capable of bringing an effective claim on behalf of the affiliate.

19. Negotiation in practice

This chapter imagines a hypothetical scenario, which will help to show how the negotiation approaches outlined in this book may work out in practice.

1. Background

Big Bank plc (Big Bank) is a UK based financial institution, in the area of retail banking. It is focused upon re-engineering its business processes and customer offerings so as to reflect the changing demands of the market, and in particular the shift towards mobile banking and digitisation. In this regard, it has initiated a major programme called Project Pegasus, which it expects to result in the digital transformation of its business and to put it in a better competitive position against both its traditional rivals and the new challengers, both banks and fintechs.

Project Pegasus has many different streams to it; some relate to re-engineering its underlying infrastructure so as to make it more resilient, flexible and easier to upgrade (and involving a shift of many of its legacy applications and infrastructure into a hybrid public/private cloud model). Others relate to the implementation of new solutions which are better suited to the perceived future requirements of Big Bank, being a mix of on premise and software as a service (SaaS) solutions. Big Bank will also be outsourcing a number of supporting functions (such as service desk, finance and accounting, HR and workforce management, etc), and the service providers it appoints for such outsourced operations will need to have access to many of the new solutions in order to provide their envisaged services to Big Bank.

SuperTech Limited (SuperTech) is a well-known and multinational technology service provider, headquartered in the US but with substantial operations throughout Europe and a major back office/service delivery function in India. It is particularly well known for its customer relationship management (CRM) solution called CustomerFirst, which it offers to clients on the basis of a SaaS subscription model. SuperTech also provides extensive consultancy services to its clients so as to assist with the configuration of CustomerFirst to meet the client's particular requirements, the creation of interfaces with the client's other applications and services and change management so as to help the client adjust its operations and processes to fit in with the capabilities and modes of operation of CustomerFirst.

Big Bank is considering implementing CustomerFirst as part of the overall jigsaw of Project Pegasus.

2. Initial considerations

From the perspective of Big Bank, there will be a number of immediate questions which its lawyers/negotiating team will need to ask, including, in particular, the following.

- Have the capabilities of CustomerFirst been fully tested and understood, or will this be part of the process going forward?
- What are the key drivers for Big Bank? For example, is the functionality and technical capability of the solution the overwhelming point of importance, or is it more a question of getting the most cost-effective solution?
- What are the timescales that Big Bank is operating to? Is there, for example, an existing CRM system or solution which needs to be replaced or which is coming to the end of a defined contract term? Or, are there any cross dependencies with other aspects of Project Pegasus which would be impacted by any delay in choosing and implementing the new CRM system?
- Are there any other bidders still 'in play' as competition to SuperTech, and how strong are their offerings perceived to be, in comparison to CustomerFirst?

The answers to these kinds of questions will then enable Big Bank's negotiating team to help find focus with their drafting of the contract, and also inform them as to the strength (or otherwise) of their bargaining position.

SuperTech, on the other hand, will have some different questions in mind, which will include the following.

- How close a 'fit' is CustomerFirst perceived to be for Big Bank's requirements? For example, would the transaction be primarily about the provision of a commodity style SaaS offering with limited additional services, or will the engagement be more bespoke and services led?
- Who is the competition and how cogent are they believed to be? There may be a limited appetite to expend substantial effort and cost in pursuing an opportunity where SuperTech

may be little more than a stalking horse for an alternative supplier or solution.

- What is the potential value of the opportunity? If the size of the deal is not substantial, the willingness to expend significant time and effort in considering amendments to SuperTech's own standard terms may be somewhat limited. If, however, the deal is more substantial, then there will be a greater likelihood not just of detailed negotiation, but also a debate in the first instance as to whose contract terms are to form the basis for the commencement of such negotiations.

3. The procurement process

3.1 Number of bidders

The first question for Big Bank to consider is how many bidders it wants to send its request for proposal (RfP) out to, and then how many bidders it will select to engage in negotiation.

Initially, Big Bank will want to ensure that it canvases a sufficient number of bidders to ensure that it has a good idea of what the market has to offer, and which potential suppliers might therefore be best suited to its requirements. Having multiple bidders also provides Big Bank with leverage, on the basis that the competing suppliers will have a powerful motivation to make concessions (eg, if they know that Big Bank has readily available alternatives) and also Big Bank has the ability to play one bidder off against another, for example by pointing out that Supplier A is at odds with the rest of the bidders if they are taking a particular adverse position which the others are not (although it should be cautioned that the overall confidentiality of the bidding process needs to be borne in mind here).

However, Big Bank has to balance this against the reality of its available resources; assessing the submissions of multiple parties will inevitably take more time and resource, and if external third parties are being engaged to assist with this process (be that external legal advisers or other specialist procurement consultants etc), it will come at an additional cost too.

SuperTech has a particular interest in the number of other bidders as well. If it is thinking strategically about the overall process, it will be weighing up its chances of success against the costs of engaging in the bidding process; if it appears that Big Bank is going to be engaging with an excessive number of potential suppliers for too long a time frame, a potentially cogent bidder may decide that the process is simply not worth engaging in, as it will end up burning through too much time and cost of its own, with an insufficient chance of success at the end of the process to justify it. Instead, SuperTech may be better advised to then put its resources towards alternative bids, even if they are on the face of them for smaller sums (but with greater chances of success).

3.2   Request for proposal

When the RfP documentation goes out, it should ideally have enough information within it so as to enable the bidders to appreciate fully what it is that is entailed, and what its scope is likely to involve. There is little to be gained in sending out a document which is incomplete or set at too high a level, as the questions will inevitably arise at some point and need to be answered, and so putting in the effort up front will not involve any wasted endeavours or cost.

Linked to this is the preparation of the due diligence and background information which will underpin the RfP and the project itself. This will include such things as historic performance details *vis-à-vis* any services which are to be passed over to a successful bidder for an outsource-style transaction, details of relevant third party agreements (eg, third-party licence agreements regarding software which the successful bidder will need to access or use on behalf of the customer), and at least a high-level summary of any in-scope customer personnel (*vis-à-vis* any potential Transfer of Undertakings (Protection of Employment) Regulations 2006 (TUPE) impacts).

In this example, historic performance will be less relevant, as SuperTech will be providing a new solution. However, making sure that the RfP is clear on how SuperTech's solution is intended to interface, not just with Big Bank's existing infrastructure but also the services and solutions to now be implemented as part and parcel of Project Pegasus, is of key importance. The prospects of a TUPE transfer will also be uncertain. Although the contract is for a new SaaS solution, it could conceivably be replacing CRM-focused human effort, and so still constitute a 'transfer' of an undertaking.

3.3   Key terms versus full contract

Customers sometimes send out RfP documents which omit any reference to particular contract requirements, and instead focus solely on the technical and commercial requirements. The lawyers/legal community will typically advise against this, however, at least in relation to more substantial projects. The point that will be made in this regard is that it will be of less benefit to know what is being offered (and for who much), without also understanding the terms on which it is being offered. To take a more extreme example, an apparently attractive solution may be fatally undermined as an overall proposition if – when the contract terms finally come to be considered – it turns out that the supplier has in mind only offering it up on the basis that there is no commitment to it actually working, and no financial compensation or recompense on offer if it doesn't.

In this regard, one key choice for the customer is whether to send out a fully drafted contract (and to then require the bidders to send back a fully marked-up draft in response), or to instead issue some 'key commercial requirements', which typically set out the key contract requirements at a more high level, and may require a yes/no response from the bidders in terms of their compliance with the relevant requirement, in a similar kind of format to what may be being used with the non-contractual parts of the RfP document.

There is no absolute right or wrong choice in this regard. Typically, however, the larger/higher the value of the project, the more likely it tends to be that the customer will be issuing a full set of contract terms.

However, a further nuance comes in the context of software-based projects (as would potentially be the case with the current scenario). Where the supplier is proposing to offer a standard or commoditised product (whether in the form of an on-premise licence, or cloud-based offering), it is far more likely that they will be proposing to use their own contract documentation as the basis for negotiation, and so may be highly resistant to any suggestion in an RfP that they be required to contract on the basis of the customer's proposed contract document. In such cases, the use of a key commercial terms/requirements document may be preferable, in terms of focusing attention on those amendments to the supplier's standard terms that the customer may in any event still require.

3.4 Process to downselection

The customer will also need to decide on its process for downselecting a successful bidder. Key options in this regard would be the following.

- *Sole source from the outset.* In other words, selecting a bidder who is felt to be the ideal or logical fit, and negotiate with them alone. This can be quicker and cheaper than the other options, but necessarily entails a loss of potential bargaining leverage for the customer, and begs the question as to what will happen if the customer is not in fact able to agree acceptable terms with its identified potential supplier?

- *Sole source as from the initial RfP responses.* This does at least give the customer an initial opportunity to compare multiple bids (and potentially get some benefit from competitive leverage in terms of the contract related responses that all of the bidders may put in, when they don't know if they have been selected), but thereafter will face the same challenges as the first option, above.
- *Initial parallel negotiations with multiple bidders, with a view to progressively reducing them in number.* For example, if seven bidders respond to the RfP, four are then taken through to initial discussions/negotiations, before a shortlisting to just two or three, and with a decision then taken as to a single, preferred bidder to take through to contract finalisation). This option gives the customer a great deal more leverage during the procurement process and the ability to play each bidder off against the others, but is not without its own disadvantages. In particular, bidders may be reluctant to continue to engage in earnest with a potentially expensive bid process if there are too many competing bidders still in the frame (such that the chances of success remain uncertain), while the customer will incur more effort and cost in having to continue to engage with multiple bidders.
- *Initial parallel negotiations with at least two bidders.* As with the third option, above, here the customer proceeds all the way to having fully negotiated and drafted contracts with at least two potential suppliers, prior to making a decision as to who to sign up with. This preserves leverage right to the very end of the process (and may actually be the required process to follow in regulated procurements, for example in the public sector), but is undoubtedly the most labour intensive and expensive procurement option.

Given the nature of SuperTech's offerings and Big Bank's requirements, the third option (ie, a 'Key Commercial Terms' document) may appear to be the preferable solution in this case.

4. Key contract aspirations of the parties

Big Bank will have certain key requirements that it will need to ensure that its contract with its chosen service provider will reflect. These include the following.

- *Scope of use.* Big Bank is clearly envisaging having outsource service providers taking on a range of its internal functions.

Accordingly, when looking at the provisions in the contract regarding scope of use or access to its selected solution, they will need to ensure that they allow for use by third parties who need to have access to the solution for the purposes of their own service delivery to Big Bank.

- *Timeliness.* Project Pegasus would appear to have a degree of time pressure associated with it, and may very well also have interfaces and dependencies with other streams/services, other than the solution which SuperTech is bidding to provide. Big Bank may, accordingly, look to include provisions in the contract to help incentivise on time completion of the implementation, configuration and/or customisation of its selected solution (such as deferring payment of as much of the contract payments as possible until stated milestones have been met, and/or having liquidated damages payable if they are late).

- *Acceptance.* Big Bank will want to have an opportunity to test fully the proposed solution so as to ensure that it does in fact perform as expected (which may include non-functional requirements such as scalability and response times). Therefore, it will want to avoid 'deemed' acceptance provisions or standard service provider provisions to the effect that the solution is automatically accepted upon delivery or installation.

- *Warranties and service levels.* In order to ensure that there are some 'teeth' to the promises being made by its chosen service provider, Big Bank will want to try to include a detailed set of warranties and associated service levels, so as to have a clear contractual commitment from its supplier to ensure that the solution does in fact work as anticipated.

- *Liability.* In the same vein as with warranty and service levels, Big Bank will want to know that it has some meaningful recourse in the event that things do not, in fact, turn out as planned. On that basis, it will want; firstly, to have as many types of loss as possible kept outside the liability regime; secondly, to know where there are types of loss that are to be subject to any kind of cap and to have such cap set as high as possible; and, thirdly, to minimise the scope of any list of losses which are simply excluded absolutely.

SuperTech of course will have some different priorities. Their key concerns are likely to focus upon the following.

- *Big Bank responsibilities.* The implementation of any new solution is likely to require the provision of both information and assistance by Big Bank, and SuperTech will want to make sure that Big Bank is therefore committed to provide such information and assistance.
- *Scope.* Given that technology projects have a tendency to drift/expand in terms of the requirements of users, SuperTech will want to ensure that the scope of its obligations is clearly delineated (so that it has the opportunity to raise a change request – and be appropriately compensated – should the scope change).
- *Payment.* SuperTech will be entering into its arrangement with Big Bank for commercial reward, and so inevitably will have a clear focus on the payment-related provisions. Aside from how much is payable, SuperTech will want to ensure that, firstly, time for payment of invoices is as short as possible; secondly, it can recover interest (and potentially suspend services or terminate the contract) should payment be made late; and, thirdly, there is a clear mechanism for altering the charges where necessary, eg, in the case of change or to reflect the impact of inflation on charges which extend across longer time periods.
- *Protection of Intellectual Property (IP).* SuperTech's 'crown jewels' lie in the IP rights which subsist in its solution, and so it will be keen to ensure that these are fully protected. This will include by way of, firstly, clearly restricting Big Bank's scope of permitted use, and, secondly, inserting appropriate prohibitions upon access to SuperTech's confidential or proprietary materials (eg, to any of their competitors).
- *Risk.* All suppliers see contractual requirements for projects such as this as incorporating a balance of risk and reward. SuperTech will, accordingly, want to ensure that the combination of the default-related provisions in the contract (such as delay payments/liquidated damages, service credits, limits of liability etc) do not create an overall degree of risk which is disproportionate to the reward that SuperTech is due to receive in the form of its charges.
- *Employees.* If SuperTech's pricing has not included the potential cost of either employing or making redundant any staff of Big Bank who may assert TUPE-related rights to transfer their contracts of employment to SuperTech, SuperTech will want the contract to assign all such related costs to Big Bank.

5. Likely areas for key debate and potential solutions

5.1 Acceptance process

The fact that there will need to be some kind of acceptance process will not be contentious. It is likely to also be readily agreed that the criteria to be used in this regard should be objectively linkable back to the contract's specific requirements, rather than the subjective 'satisfaction' of Big Bank with what SuperTech has delivered.

SuperTech may argue that acceptance should be 'deemed' to have occurred if Big Bank does not complete the acceptance process within an agreed period of time. Although Big Bank may initially resist this, it may ultimately agree to this provided that, firstly, the initial acceptance period is long enough, and, secondly, there is a 'reminder' process and period (eg, to guard against the risk that a required approver is simply unavailable or ill, etc).

5.2 Timeliness of delivery

Big Bank may start aggressively by both back-ending payments and requiring the payment of liquidated damages in the event of delays in milestones being met. The extent to which it sticks to such a position may depend upon its assessment of the knock-on impact of delay upon its business. Are there, for example, known dependencies (and linked costs) to other projects? Or are there known cost savings which would be negatively impacted by project delays?

For its part, SuperTech will likely argue that simply holding back significant elements of the payments due to it, pending upon identified milestones being met, will itself provide it with ample incentivisation to focus on on-time delivery (given the fact that if there is an ongoing delay, it will also likely be incurring additional delivery related costs and expenses of its own).

The potential compromises that may then end up being negotiated would be:

- varying the degree of payments that will be kept back to the end of the project (eg, if there are no liquidated damages payable in the event of delay, then a greater percentage of payment will be deferred);
- Where there are liquidated damages payable, the parties may negotiate an initial 'grace period' of delay when no such sanction will apply, and that thereafter the liquidated damages only gradually 'ramp up' in line with the worsening delay (eg, £X might be payable for the first week/part week of

delay, two times £X for the second week/part week, two point five times £X for the third week/part week, etc); or

- the liquidated damages may be expressed as a sole remedy for delay, at least during the period while the liquidated damages are accruing.

5.3 Warranty/service level agreement provisions

Had SuperTech's solution been an on-premise software licence, a key area of debate would have been the length of the relevant warranty that the software would conform with its applicable specification. For an SaaS solution this should not be an issue (as the support services to ensure that this remains the case are in effect bundled up with the overall charges), but that simply switches the focus of the parties onto the related service level provisions.

SuperTech would ideally have service level expressed more as targets or on an aspirational basis, ie, such that there is no immediate contractual sanction in the event that they are not met. Given the importance of a solution such as CustomerFirst to Big Bank's operations, however, Big Bank would be less likely to accept such a position.

Accordingly, it would be likely that the parties would negotiate that there are binding service levels; the negotiations would instead focus upon:

- the levels that are then agreed to be achieved (eg, in terms of the availability of the solution, time to remedy particular types of incidents etc);
- the amount of SuperTech's charges that will be placed 'at risk' to the payment of service credits; and
- whether the service credits are to be a 'sole remedy' so as to preclude Big Bank from also recovering damages (which would be a difficult position for Big Bank to accept, albeit that it might consider some kind of additional threshold before such claims can be made, eg, that a set proportion of the at risk amount be incurred, or the service level breach in question be at a particularly bad level).

5.4 Liability clauses

It is near inevitable that Big Bank and SuperTech would end up with potentially lengthy negotiations as to the liability provisions. The nature of the implementation of CustomerFirst is that Big Bank could not see it simply as a low-risk commodity style product, and would instead also need to factor in the potential risks associated with configuration and implementation, where there would be ample scope for things to go wrong and to impact upon Big Bank's operations.

Knowing that these risks exist, SuperTech will be no less inclined to try to reduce or manage its risks associated with the project. It may, for example, seek to argue that the configuration and implementation effort is in effect a separate endeavour from the ongoing charges associated with the SaaS service thereafter, so as to create a ring-fenced liability cap associated with the initial setup and implementation, and a separate cap for the delivery of the SaaS service thereafter.

Aside from the negotiation of the cap itself, other facets of the liability regime which would in this case be particular focuses for the negotiation would include the following.

- *Data protection liabilities*. The fact that CustomerFirst is a CRM solution means that it is a certainty that personal data will be in view, and as such the parties will end up debating whether personal data related claims will be unlimited or (more likely) subject to some level of 'super cap' outside of the normal limits of liability.
- *Regulatory fines*. Financial institutions such as Big Bank have the added concern of being subject to fines by their regulators in the event of technology-related failures. Big Bank may again argue that such liabilities should sit outside the limits of liability, while SuperTech will be nervous that the quantum of any such fines may in any event be exacerbated by past issues or failings of Big Bank and its technology infrastructure which are unrelated to SuperTech.
- *The scope of the exclusions*. SuperTech will undoubtedly argue hard that it cannot take on liability for loss of profit, in particular to the usual exclusions of indirect or consequential loss. While this is not an unusual stance, the nature of the CustomerFirst solution and the fact that it is likely to be directly customer impacting may make Big Bank less willing to accept such a position. Potential compromises may then involve having some kind of liquidated damages or 'super service credit' remedy for issues which might arise and impact upon Big Bank's profits, or possibly to allow loss of profit to be claimable if it is a direct loss, but subject to a (lower) sub-cap within the overall limits of liability.
- *The scope of deemed direct loss*. Given the wider nature of Project Pegasus and the possibility that defaults by SuperTech in the

implementation of CustomerFirst may impact upon other suppliers to or aspects of Project Pegasus, Big Bank may seek to ensure that such losses/impacts are included within a list of 'deemed' direct losses, and so as to avoid SuperTech from arguing in the future that they should be excluded altogether by reason of being a form or indirect loss. SuperTech may ultimately be willing to agree to this, provided that the losses in question are still 'caused' by them, are reasonably incurred, and subject to a general obligation of mitigation.

Quite where the parties end up on all of these key points (and on the negotiation as a whole) will depend on a number of factors. These will include the following.

- *The bargaining leverage of the parties.* How desperate is Big Bank for the CustomerFirst solution, or is SuperTech to win Big Bank as a client and earn the charges associated with the project?
- *The relationship between the parties.* If there is an existing and/ or amicable relationship between them, compromises and concessions may be easier to find.
- *The skills and market knowledge of the negotiation teams.* A cohesive and experienced negotiation team will always be likely to gain a better overall result than one which is poorly coordinated and/or not well versed in the 'art of the possible'.
- *The procurement process selected.* Are there for example still other bidders in the process whose positions on outstanding contract issues can be compared with those of SuperTech (so as to either convince Big Bank that SuperTech is in fact being reasonable and acting in line with the wider market or encourage Big Bank to press for concessions that other suppliers seem willing to make).

20. Conclusion

We hope that as you come to the end of this book, you will feel better equipped for your future endeavours in negotiating technology-related contracts. As we hope will have become clear, there is invariably no intrinsic right or wrong answer to the questions which such negotiations can throw up. The best adviser will not necessarily be the brightest person in the room, but will very often be the person who has the most experience and the best grasp of what is within 'the art of the possible', in terms of alternative positions and how they fit with market norms.

However, even with such knowledge stored away, the negotiation process is fundamentally dependent upon leverage, and bargaining strength. If you are fortunate enough to be the negotiating party who has something which the other side desperately wants and has few (if any) options to get from anywhere else, then you can expect to achieve a far better outcome from the negotiation process. Equally, if you are coming to the negotiation table from a position of weakness, the whole process can feel especially daunting and exhausting, and will often devolve into more of an exercise of damage limitation.

The first step in any negotiation process should, accordingly, be to try to work out just where you stand in terms of respective negotiating powers.

From a customer perspective, the kind of questions you might ask would include the following.

- How much is the deal worth?
- How many other potential providers of the relevant goods or services are there?
- What stage has the process reached? For example, this could be just going out to the market to seek expressions of interest, or – as more of a worse case – the service provider having already been selected, and contract terms now being discussed for the first time.
- What is Plan B if a deal cannot be negotiated?

Service providers might ask similar questions, but also consider other factors such as the following.

- Who else is bidding for the work?
- How well do we know the customer entity, and/or do we have a good track record with them?
- How are our products/services perceived in the market place in general? For example, are we are market leader or relatively unknown?

Knowing your comparative position *vis-à-vis* the other party will then help to inform your approach in the negotiation process. For example, an aggressive approach based on talking loudly and banging on the table will not likely yield dividends when the other party feels that it has the balance of power very firmly in its own hands. In such circumstances, an approach based on empathy and the need to maintain relationships will be more likely to produce a fruitful outcome.

The nature of the deal itself will also be an essential factor. For a one-off purchase arrangement such as the acquisition of technology equipment or a licence, the future relationship of the parties will be less of a consideration and the parties can accordingly feel more free to negotiate 'hard' to get the best possible outcome in terms of transfer of risk and cost to the other party. Where, however, the deal involves the parties in a longer-term or continuing relationship (as will particularly be the case with multi-year, outsource-style relationships, for example), an approach of negotiating to 'win' each and every point on the contract may end up creating longer-term friction between the parties or even serve to create a somewhat 'brittle' deal, which will be more prone to future renegotiation to the potential detriment of both parties. In such circumstances the contract negotiators would be well advised to remember that what constitutes success in those situations is a contract which will support the longer-term delivery of the services as envisaged by the commercial parties, rather than one which is more overtly slanted in terms of obligations or remedies in favour of one party as opposed to the other.

We want to note that the negotiation marketplace is also dynamic, and particularly so in the world of technology-related contracts. What may have appeared to be normal or market standard at one time will not necessarily remain so forever, and contract drafting and expected negotiation outcomes may change accordingly. The switch in approach to the setting of liability caps in relation to claims relating to personal data is one more recent example of this, but past examples of development of contract drafting include the growth in the use of 'relief notice' style provisions, the increasing incidence of liability provisions allowing for a measure of recovery of loss of profit or revenue, and the application of transitional use provisions to software licences and software as a service (SaaS) agreements, running alongside whatever they may say about rights of termination. Any future editions of this book therefore will likely need considerable updating to reflect such market dynamics, as well as to address the new issues that will inevitably be thrown up by contracts to deal with new technological developments to do with, for example, artificial intelligence or blockchain.

We wish you every success with your future contracting endeavours.

Kit Burden
Mark O'Conor
Duncan Pithouse
DLA Piper

About the authors

Kit Burden
Partner, DLA Piper
kit.burden@dlapiper.com

Kit Burden is a partner at DLA Piper and is co-head of its global Technology Sector. He has been advising clients in relation to technology and sourcing mandates for nearly 30 years, and is involved in projects and with clients in jurisdictions all around the world. He acts for both major buy-side and sell-side clients, including some of the best-known organisations in the technology sector and many household-name brands. He has been awarded numerous accolades over the years, including Legal Advisor of the Year (Global Sourcing Association), UK Technology Lawyer of the Year (Legal Experts), and Strategic Advisor of the Year (Global Sourcing Association) and has for many years been listed in Tier 1 for IT and outsourcing matters in both the *Legal 500* and *Chambers* legal directories. He is the co-author and editor of three previous books on IT contracts, legal protection of computer software and outsourcing, published respectively by Sweet and Maxwell, EMIS and Globe.

Mark O'Conor
Partner, DLA Piper
mark.oconor@dlapiper.com

Mark O'Conor is a partner at DLA Piper and heads its Client Group for the London office, as well as being a past managing partner of the UK firm. He started his career at Bird and Bird before moving to DLA Piper, where he has practised for the last 15 years. He works with a diverse set of clients in both the private and public sectors, including a wide range of household name organisations. He has also had a long-standing involvement with the Society for Computers and Law (SLC), and is the current chair of the board of trustees for the SCL. He is a frequent speaker and writer on technology and legal themes and is listed in both *Chambers* and *Legal 500* as a leading technology lawyer.

Duncan Pithouse
Partner, DLA Piper
duncan.pithouse@dlapiper.com

Duncan Pithouse is a partner in the London office of DLA Piper, and heads the UK Technology and Sourcing Group. His focus is on technology contracts and outsourcing agreements, with a particular focus upon work in highly regulated sectors such as banking and insurance. He is a frequent contributor of articles and thought leadership on technology legal matters, and is recognised as a leading practitioner in the various legal directories. His clients include some of the world's largest financial services institutions and insurance companies.

Index

About Globe Law and Business

Globe Law and Business was established in 2005, and from the very beginning, we set out to create law books which are sufficiently high level to be of real use to the experienced professional, yet still accessible and easy to navigate. Most of our authors are drawn from Magic Circle and other top commercial firms, both in the UK and internationally.

Our titles are carefully produced, with the utmost attention paid to editorial, design and production processes. We hope this results in high-quality books which are easy to read, and a pleasure to own. All our new books are also available as ebooks, which are compatible with most desktop, laptop and tablet devices.

We have recently expanded our portfolio to include a new range of journals, Special Reports and Good Practice Guides, available both digitally and in hard copy format, and produced to the same high standards as our books.

We'd very much like to hear from you with your thoughts and ideas for improving what we offer. Please do feel free to email me at sian@globelawandbusiness.com with your views.

Sian O'Neill
Managing director
Globe Law and Business

www.globelawandbusiness.com